HAUNTED
LIVERPOOL 2

For the Merseymart Girls
Gail and Jenny
Also for Jim Brakell, for taking a chance.
And last but not least, a big thanks to the gang at the studio:
Roy Corlett, Alec Young and Billy Butler.

Published by The Bluecoat Press, Liverpool
Book design by March Design, Liverpool
Front cover illustration and photograph by Angela Mounsey
Printed by D2P

ISBN 1 872568 77 7

Tom Slemen
HAUNTED
LIVERPOOL 2

The Bluecoat Press

Contents

4

Introduction

The Truth-seekers' battle goes on day and night.
Kabir

As I stated in the introduction to *Haunted Liverpool 1*, science no longer holds any absolute truths. It has even been found to be hopelessly inadequate in explaining such elemental forces as gravity and light. Therefore, how can we expect scientists to unravel the mysteries within this book?

With the exception of Edinburgh University, which has a department that studies the paranormal, and a couple of universities in the USA, there are no government funded projects in the United Kingdom to look into ghosts and other psychic phenomena.

I recently wrote to David Canter, Professor of Psychology at Liverpool University, asking why there is no Chair of Parapsychology at the university. The reply I received, which was written on his behalf, was both amusing and typical:

Dear Tom,
Your query on parapsychology has reached me. You should realise that the Edinburgh Department is the only one of its kind in Europe and, in fact, I only know of one other department, which is in the USA. You should appreciate that the reason very few psychologists are interested in ghosts and the like is because over 100 years of study has shown that although these phenomena tell us something about the person who experiences them, they tell us nothing about the spirit world. So, if at any point you wanted a psychologist to explain what people were experiencing, I am sure we could find one.

All the best,
I McIntosh,
(pp David Canter)

In other words, people who see ghosts need their heads examining. It is infuriating to think that we are paying taxes so that the government can give a hefty wage packet to myopic people of this sort, who live in their ivory towers. If people who see ghosts are insane, we must include Her Majesty the Queen, who, with her husband, Prince Phillip and Princess Alexandra, has attended many séances and seen her late father, King George VI.

Then there is the famous psychologist, Carl Gustav Jung, the founder of Jungian psychology, who saw a ghostly head resting on a pillow next to his when he was in bed one night. It is also said that US Presidents, Kennedy and Roosevelt, both saw the spectre of President Lincoln on several occasions in the White House. In his fascinating book, *X-Rated: The Paranormal Secrets of the Stars*, author Michael Munn informs us that many showbiz stars have had spooky encounters, including celebrities like Liverpool-born star, Cilla Black, one of the highest-paid entertainers on British television.

Munn explains how Cilla has seen the ghost of a teenaged girl, standing by her bed, on several occasions over a period of seven years. When the visitations first happened, Cilla thought that one of her children had come into the room, but when she looked up, she saw what she described as "a sweet-looking young girl standing there, wearing a long old-fashioned dress". Amazingly, Cilla did not feel at all frightened of the apparition. In fact she claimed that she actually liked her being there. She has tried to speak to the ghost on several occasions, but she never looks at her or answers her questions. Instead, she just smiles and floats away through the door.

Munn also mentions other highly successful celebrities who have seen ghosts or had psychic experiences; people like Madonna, Roger Moore, Telly Savalas, Peter Sellers, Tommy Steele and Sir Alec Guinness to name just a few. I am sure that most of these celebrities would be very angry if Liverpool University's Mr McIntosh told them that the things they had seen were all in the mind.

It was recently discovered that if you hammer two nails into a stone wall, then wire the nails to the microphone socket of a domestic tape recorder, you can sometimes record mysterious and inexplicable sounds, potentially related to the supernatural. This intriguing experiment has been carried out in buildings where ghostly phenomena have been reported over the years and indeed phantom voices have been recorded. It seems that the stone walls of many residences that are reputedly haunted contain silica, ferric oxide and quartz, which may act as a natural tape recorder.

Ferric oxide is the brown material that cassette tapes are partly made of and it seems to be the main culprit. It is as though when the stones are slightly compressed, perhaps through temperature changes, the quartz generates what is known as piezo-electricity, which is a way of producing electrical energy by applying pressure to a crystal. When you click some electric lighters, the blue ignition spark is produced by the pressure you have exerted on a small piece of piezo-electric crystal. When this piezo-electricity flows through the stone wall, it powers up the audio recordings in the stone's ferric oxide, in turn producing sounds. It is an exciting breakthrough in the study of ghosts and may eventually explain how ghostly sounds become recorded in rock.

In this book I mention several mysterious disappearances (*Spirited Away and Into Thin Air*). The cause of these disappearances may well be supernatural, yet I suspect that they are merely cases of a phenomenon known in the occult world as 'teleportation'.

In the 1950s, the pioneering UFO writer, MK Jessup, unearthed a peculiar story from the archives of Spain's legal records, which concerned the trial of a Spanish guard named Gil Perez. Perez had allegedly been on duty at the Governor's Palace in Manila on 25 October 1593, when he suddenly found himself in the main square of Mexico City. His dramatic appearance from nowhere naturally alarmed the passers-by and the guard quickly attracted the attention of the Mexican authorities. Perez was unable to explain how he had been transported instantaneously thousands of miles across the globe from the Philippines.

The only details he could supply amounted to vague descriptions and a garbled account of a mysterious cloud, which enveloped him moments before his trip, but he could remember nothing more. Perez stated that the sinister incident had occurred minutes after the assassination of the Manilan Governor and three months later, a ship from the Philippines reached Mexico and confirmed the assassination and other details of the soldier's story. In such a superstitious age, Perez was lucky not to have been burnt at the stake.

However, such was the fate of a man in 1655 who was deemed to be a black magician by the Spanish Inquisition because he was inexplicably transported from the Portuguese colony in Goa, India, to Portugal, in the proverbial twinkling of an eye.

The famed student of the unexplained, Charles Fort (1874-1932) was intrigued by a plethora of reports, gleaned from newspaper cuttings and historical records, of people who had somehow been transferred from one place to another without any physical movement through the usual three dimensions of space. Fort coined the term 'teleportation' to describe this bizarre phenomenon, a word which is now only found in the pages of science-fiction. That, of course, does not debase the concept of teleportation. Television, computers, lasers and the atom bomb were also only words in science-fiction literature until not so long ago.

The logic of cybernetics suggests that every physical object can, in principle, be reduced to encoded information which could be transmitted on a carrier wave. This may seem a little far-fetched, but the idea of compressing Beethoven's works onto a compact disc and the technology of a home computer would seem equally unbelievable to your Victorian counterpart; it is just a matter of time and technological progress. Today we can send television pictures, radio bulletins and faxes anywhere in the world via satellite; tomorrow we may be able to actually send ourselves in a similar way. But how will such a feat of technology be achieved? There are two areas of science which may provide the breakthrough in teleportation – electronics and theoretical physics.

Electronics is progressing at an alarming rate. In 1948, the invention of the transistor was hailed as a quantum leap in technology and its inventors were awarded the Nobel Prize for their work, but there are now tiny silicon chips, in common use, which contain over 18 million transistors. These chips are becoming more complex each year. Let us imagine a time in the not too distant future when we will have chips that are complex enough to store and process the exact positions of every atom in the human body. There are around 5×10^{27} atoms in your body, which may seem a staggering figure, but there are mainframe computers in existence that could easily handle such a sum. Now, if we can envisage a device that could scan the human body atom by atom and store the positions of each atom on our super-computer chips, we are halfway to constructing a teleporter.

Along these lines, a similar body-scanner is routinely used in hospitals and works by the principle of nuclear magnetic resonance. In such hospital scanners, the atoms in the patient's body are mapped by a computer and presented on a screen in a series of cross sections. The problem is, of course, translating the information in our scanner back into atoms, for this formidable task we would need something along the lines of a particle accelerator, which could convert basic atoms of hydrogen (the simplest atom) into the various carbon, nitrogen and other atoms of which we are made.

This hypothetical 'matter transmitter' would also be an advanced duplicating machine, because it would merely copy the original person atom by atom. To be a true teleporter, our machine would have to actually transfer the original subject to a destination and, in theory, this could be achieved by warping the very fabric of space. Two of the greatest geniuses of the 20th century – Albert Einstein and Professor John A Wheeler (co-inventor of the H-Bomb), have claimed that space can be distorted and bent by gravity and high-density magnetic fields to provide a form of instantaneous transportation across superspace.

According to Wheeler, superspace is another form of space which runs alongside our own, but it does not have time as we know it. As long ago as 1927, Einstein had reached a similar conclusion. That year he completed a paper entitled 'Unified Field Theory for Gravitation and Electricity'. Shortly after the theory was published in Germany, the paper was suddenly withdrawn from circulation. In the scientific community there were rumours that Einstein had withdrawn his paper because he thought that his work was too far ahead of its time and feared that the military powers of pre-Nazi Germany would abuse it.

After World War II (and the horrors of Hiroshima and Nagasaki) the pacifist philosopher, Bertrand Russell – a close friend of Einstein – read Einstein's secret paper on the Unified Field Theory. Lord Russell enigmatically remarked that mankind was not ready for such a far-reaching theory. Others who have read Einstein's intriguing paper claim that he had formulated ground-breaking equations, showing that magnetism and gravity were related and also how space could be distorted with high-powered magnetic fields in such a way as to provide instant travel to any point on this earth or away from it.

If Einstein's theory is correct, how would it explain the teleportation of Gil Perez in 1593? No one in those times would have possessed the technology to generate space-warping magnetic fields. Perhaps nature herself may have been the culprit. The source of the earth's magnetic field is still a complete mystery, but satellite surveys of the geomagnetic field have revealed a host of hitherto unknown magnetic storms – localised points on the earth's surface where the earth's magnetic field becomes very intense for a matter of minutes. Most of these storms occur at sea, but some have formed on land and have actually disrupted radio communications.

Perhaps Gil Perez was in the eye of one of these storms in 1593. If so, perhaps the Spanish guard was transported across the world via Professor Wheeler's superspace. The magnetic-storm theory would also explain the disappearances in the Bermuda Triangle, where many of the final radio messages from lost ships and planes mention disorientation because of a spinning magnetic compass.

So much for teleportation; what technology would we use for contacting or detecting ghosts? Have you noticed that no matter how sophisticated an alarm system is today, something always seems to trigger it? Most households nowadays are fitted with basic burglar alarms which are activated when anything moves in the vicinity of their infra-red passive detectors. These alarms are becoming something of a national menace according to statistics from various noise pollution groups, so what is causing them to go off? The answer may well be ghosts.

An excellent example is the case of an alarm that went off at the Butterflies nightclub in Oldham around 1997. Police raced to what they thought was either a break-in or a faulty alarm. When they arrived at the premises, they found no sign of a break-in or anyone in the place. However, when they looked closely at the videotape from the security cameras, they were intrigued to see the shape of a youth in a white t-shirt walking down a corridor. The figure appeared to be semi-transparent. It even seemed to pass straight through a closed locked door, when the alarm went off. The owners of the club believe that the spectre is the ghost of an electrician who was fatally electrocuted during a rewiring job at the club many years ago.

8

Such cases seem to indicate that ghosts can trigger infra-red alarms, but could there be some other way we can detect them? I believe the answer lies in the plant kingdom. This idea will probably be ridiculed, but here goes. In February 1965, Cleve Baxter, a former CIA employee and one of the leading experts in lie-detection, discovered that if he connected his polygraph (lie detector) electrodes to the leaves of one of his houseplants and watered it, the trace on his pen recorder did not record an increase in the electrical conductivity of the plant. This amazed him, because it seemed to run against the basic laws of electrical resistance.

The trace on his machine instead showed a pattern of steadily decreasing conductivity, which seemed to indicate that the plant was undergoing a relaxing experience when it was watered. This finding encouraged Baxter to conduct further experiments with the plant. When he merely thought about burning a leaf of the wired-up plant with his lighter, the pen of the polygraph recorder made a sharp upward jump. To Baxter, there seemed to be only one possible but incredible explanation – the plant was somehow reading his mind!

To discount the possibility that his polygraph was faulty, or that the plant reaction was some kind of anomaly, he also tested hundreds of other plants, using many different models of polygraphs; the results were always the same, the plants seemed to possess some sort of consciousness. There is still experimental work being carried out on Baxter's findings, but scientists are unable to agree on how, or why, plants exhibit psycho-galvanic readings when they are wired up. It is now known, and widely accepted, however, that plants certainly are able to respond to certain kinds of music and human speech.

An excellent example is the renowned nurseryman Luther Burbank, of Santa Rosa, California, who spent many years at the turn of the century developing a new variety of spineless cactus. When botanists asked him how he had managed to produce such a species of plant, Burbank calmly replied that he talked them. "I say to them, 'you have nothing to fear. You don't need your defensive thorns. I will protect you'," was Burbank's controversial reply.

Another botany expert who has proved that plants are capable of directly responding to stimuli is Jagadis Chandra Bose, the professor of physics at Presidency College, Calcutta. Bose built a device to amplify the microscopic movement of plant tissue. He discovered that plants feel pain, as well as also exhibiting emotional responses as complex as those of a human being. In 1917 Bose was knighted for his work and in 1920 he was made a Fellow of the Royal Society. Later in the 1960s, several experimenters at the University of Ottawa showed that seedlings exposed to sound, grew more quickly when the sound was high-pitched. In the experiment, African Violets were placed next to the loudspeakers of a hi-fi system and it was found that they tended to lean away from the speaker if the music being played was rock 'n' roll, but the music of Haydn, Bach and sitar musicians made them lean towards the speaker and also to grow faster. You can easily try this simple experiment out on your own plants!

If plants are as highly sensitive as Baxter and the other far-sighted botanists are suggesting, they would make ideal sensors if they were wired to a polygraph and placed within a haunted dwelling. Perhaps any psychic activity that is not perceptible to us could be detected by the plants. It is just an idea. Anyway, do read on and enjoy the following stories from my cabinet of curiosities.

Maritime Mysteries

Brunel's Jinxed Supership

Mariners are renowned for their superstitions. To the seafarer, the sight of an albatross over a ship is a warning of an approaching storm and, as Coleridge recounted in *The Rime of the Ancient Mariner*, to kill such a bird would bring an eternity of bad luck. Even today there are fishermen who will stay ashore if they happen to meet a priest or a nun on the way to join their ship. There are still some old seadogs who will refuse to set foot on board a ship which has had its name changed, a superstition that is said to date back to 1867, when a Nova Scotian brigantine called the *Amazon* was renamed the *Marie Celeste*. The rechristened ship suffered a catalogue of calamities and was finally found abandoned, drifting near the Azores in 1872. To this day, no one knows what became of her crew.

Sailors are also extremely wary about unlucky cargoes. When an allegedly ominous mummy of the Ancient Egyptian princess, Ammon-Ra, was transferred from the British Museum into the hold of a famous liner in April 1912, many seamen were convinced that their vessel would be jinxed. It may have been sheer coincidence, but the same liner sank on her maiden voyage. She was the *Titanic*.

Another ship which had an unlucky maiden voyage was the 2000-ton steel bark *Hinemoa*. During her voyage of 1892, four apprentice seamen died of typhoid. Then the captain later went insane. The second captain of the bark turned into a ruthless thief and ended up in prison, the third became an alcoholic, the fourth died of natural causes in his cabin and the fifth committed suicide by blowing his brains out. The sixth captain of the *Hinemoa* survived the jinxed ship but, under his command, the vessel capsized and two sailors were swept to their deaths when the ship eventually righted itself. Finally, in 1908, the ship became a write-off when she drifted ashore on the west cost of Scotland. An engineer who worked on the ship firmly believed that it had been jinxed as a result of using tons of soil from an East London graveyard as ballast.

Without a doubt, the unluckiest ship that ever sailed was built at the yards of John Scott Russell in Milwall, London, over a period of three years in the late 1850s. The *Great Eastern* was the brainchild of one of the greatest engineers of all time; Isambard Kingdom Brunel. At 19,000 tons, the gigantic vessel was the most ambitious engineering project of the 19th century. The colossal 692-foot long, iron-plated, double hull of Brunel's supership surpassed the dimensions of Noah's fabled Ark and she was capable of carrying 4000 passengers.

The ship which the maritime world called the 'Wonder of the Seas' sported an unheard-of six masts and traditional maritime nomenclature could not be applied to them, so they were referred to as Monday, Tuesday, Wednesday, Thursday, Friday and Saturday. Motive power was to be supplied by a 24-foot, steam-driven propeller, or gigantic paddle wheels and, should her steam engines fail, the ship would simply unfurl her gargantuan sails. The Herculean vessel could also stockpile enough coal to provide a journey from England to Australia and back without the need to refuel.

While the *Great Eastern* was under construction at Milwall, two hundred rivet gangs worked on the ship's novel double hull, until a staggering three million rivets had been firmly hammered into place. The outer hull was separated from the inner one by a gap of three feet. Within the hulls there was an innovative arrangement of 16 watertight bulkheads, designed to make the ship virtually unsinkable.

One day in January 1857, during the round-the-clock racket of hammering and banging, somebody noticed that one of the riveters and his apprentice were missing. The weeks passed by, but the two missing men were nowhere to be found. Another riveter, an Irishman, reported that he had heard a strange pounding noise coming from within the double hull, but no one took him seriously and he was ignored and the noises were never investigated.

The width of the River Thames at the Millwall shipyards was too narrow to allow the *Great Eastern* to be launched lengthways, so the ship had to be ushered into the river sideways; an operation that took an agonising three months, during which all kinds of technical difficulties were experienced. During this protracted procedure, Brunel became ill through overwork and worry. He was only 53 years old but looked at least 20 years older, through working for years without adequate sleep. He opened the Times newspaper one day to read, with bitterness, that the editor had dismissed his time-consuming project as a white elephant:

'There she lies on the very brink of the noble river which is to carry her to the ocean, but she will not wet her lips.'

However, the leviathan finally did 'wet her lips' on 31 January 1858, after being eased 330 feet down a slipway by buckling hydraulic jacks. Brunel himself remarked that, "Putting St Paul's to sea would have been easier!"

On the very day which the *Great Eastern* was launched, Brunel was standing on deck, unable to believe that his magnificent creation was finally about to be in service, when he suffered a massive stroke and collapsed. He remained gravely ill for the next year and a half and, on 15 September 1859, he died after hearing that a steam pipe had burst on the *Great Eastern* during her trial run to Weymouth. The massive explosion had destroyed a funnel and the searing cloud of escaping steam had boiled five stokers to death.

In a separate tragedy, at around the same time, another crewman had fallen onto a paddle wheel and been instantly smashed to pieces. Three members of the ship's crew had talked of hearing pounding noises within the hull just before the two tragedies took place.

The astronomical costs of the delayed launch – over £1 million – brought financial ruin to the Eastern Navigation Company, who had planned to employ Brunel's ship on long voyages to India and Australia. The Great Ship Company took over the project and opted instead for the quick profits of the North Atlantic run. From that point on, the unlucky career of the *Great Eastern* started in earnest. The first planned voyage to the United States in 1861 had to be cancelled because the repair work to the ship's damaged funnel and boiler took longer than expected.

The frustrated directors of the Great Ship Company were eager to get some return on their troublesome investment, so, as an interim measure, they moved the *Great Eastern* to Holyhead in Wales, to put her on display to paying sightseers. But, shortly after arriving at Holyhead, one of the fiercest gales in living memory tore in from the Irish Sea and ripped the mighty vessel from her moorings.

For 18 agonising hours she was tossed about in the coastal waters, but she rode the storm well, while other ships sank all around her, thanks to her new-fangled double hull and waterproofed bulkheads. After the gale had moved away, the *Great Eastern* was an awesome sight, as she steamed majestically from the storm-clouded horizon, back to Holyhead. However, she did not escape unscathed, as the storm had caused thousands of pounds worth of damage to the ship's grand saloon.

Three months later, the *Great Eastern's* first captain, William Harrison, the coxswain, along with the nine-year-old son of the chief purser were all drowned, when a sudden violent storm swamped their gig as they were going ashore. In the seafaring world, nothing casts a darker shadow over a ship's character than the death of a captain prior to a maiden voyage. So, when the news of the three deaths reached London, the directors of the Great Ship Company resigned immediately.

The new board of directors, eager to restore the public's confidence in the seemingly jinxed ship, announced that the *Great Eastern* would leave Southampton for New York on 9 June 1860. The voyage was a financial disaster. All the adverse publicity had earned Brunel's ship a bad reputation and people opted for the smaller, more reliable, Cunard ships. Hundreds of tickets for the *Great Eastern's* maiden voyage were printed, but when the 9 June arrived, the ship still was not ready because of technical difficulties with its engine.

Finally, on 16 June, a mere 35 passengers boarded the mammoth vessel. The new captain, who had never made an Atlantic crossing before, commanded a crew of 418. During the 12-day crossing, poor quality, economy coal caused thick, carbonaceous deposits to form on the linings of the funnel casings, which caused the engines to overheat and this, in turn, caused the main dining room area to become intolerably hot.

Despite all these problems, when the *Great Eastern* arrived in New York, she was greeted by thousands of cheering sightseers. But things soon turned sour again when some of these onlookers attempted to go on board the British ship and they were promptly told that they would have to pay a one dollar admission fee for the privilege. People who had been forced to pay the fee were determined to get their money's worth and they pocketed anything on the ship that was not bolted down for souvenirs.

It was announced that the ship was to make a two-day excursion and 2000 people were soon queueing for tickets. But the two-day outing turned into a nightmare when it was learned that only 300 beds were available. As a result of this, over a thousand passengers had to sleep on the deck, where cinders and a steady drizzle of soot from the damaged funnels rained down on them all through the night. To make matters even worse, a pipe burst in the ship's storage room, soaking the food supplies. The only foods that were salvaged were dried chicken, over-salted meat and stale biscuits and even for these unsavoury items, the passengers were charged exorbitant prices.

By the time the burst pipe had been fixed, all the ship's drinking water had leaked away. The infuriated passengers looked forward to a speedy landing, but even that failed to be straightforward; through some unaccountable navigational error, the *Great Eastern* had drifted way off course during the night and was over one hundred miles out to sea by dawn. When the ship finally reached New York, the hungry, dirty and weary passengers scrambled to disembark. Not surprisingly, when a second excursion was announced, only a handful of tickets were purchased.

New Yorkers were sorely disappointed with the steam ship, so she returned to England and even this trip was plagued by misfortune. The screw shaft gave out in mid-Atlantic and, at Milford Haven, the ship fouled the rope of a small boat and drowned two of its passengers. Hours after the tragedy, the *Great Eastern* smashed into the frigate *Blenheim*, seriously damaging the latter's hull.

In September 1861, the unfortunate liner was struck by a hurricane in mid-Atlantic. Both side paddles were ripped off by the storm, which also tore the lifeboats away from the deck and unhinged the enormous rudder. The repairs cost over £60,000. In the following year, the *Great Eastern* was steaming through Long Island Sound near New York Harbour, when the ship struck an uncharted rock, which created a gash, 83 feet long and 9 feet wide, in the outer hull. The repairs this time cost in excess of £70,000.

The ill-starred liner was put up for auction in 1864 and was bought for a mere £25,000. Her buyers put her to work as a cable layer, but bad luck still bedevilled the vessel. In 1869, she steamed from Ireland to Newfoundland, laying a telegraph cable on the seabed as she sailed, but when she was 1,186 miles out into the Atlantic, a minor accident caused the cable to snap. The severed end sank three miles to the ocean bed and all attempts to retrieve it failed.

Further commercial missions were also dogged by one disaster after another and so the ship was eventually brought back to Milford Haven and literally abandoned by her owners. For 12 years the *Great Eastern* was left to rust. By 1886, it was decided that the derelict ship (whose hull was, by this time, covered with a layer of barnacles six feet deep) was nothing but an obstacle to the shipping lines, so the dilapidated hulk was brought to Liverpool, where she was anchored in the Mersey, emblazoned with advertising signs. Brunel must have turned in his grave when his 'wonder of the seas' was exploited and cheapened in this way.

The *Great Eastern* was sold by auction by Messrs Dixon and Moore – two Liverpool businessmen – to a firm of metal dealers. Even during her final voyage to a scrapyard near Birkenhead, she was involved in a collision with a tug in the Mersey, which subsequently almost sank after sustaining heavy damage.

It was no easy task to break up the reinforced double hull of the ship, so the wreckers' iron ball was invented for the task. Three days into the formidable demolition job, the wreckers' ball smashed into the hull, dislodging a large plate. When the ball impacted into the ship again, something was seen to fall from a hole in the hull. Two demolition experts gave orders to cease work and went to investigate the object which had fallen out of the ship onto the piles of scrap at the quayside.

They were shocked to find that it was the skeleton of a man, draped in musky clothes. Another skeleton – that of a much younger male – was later found in another compartment, sandwiched between the two hulls. The skeletons were later formally identified as those of the missing riveter and his apprentice by members of their families who had travelled from Canning Town and Dagenham. Many believed that the chilling discovery explained the *Great Eastern's* jinxed history.

Long Distance Kiss

In 1863, a ship named the *City of Limerick* left New York, bound for Liverpool. Towards the end of the journey, the ship ran into a fierce North Atlantic storm which tossed the vessel about for over a week. Relatives of the crew and passengers, on both sides of the Atlantic, were naturally deeply concerned about the lives of those on board the *City of Limerick*. One of these worried people was one Mrs Wilmot in

14

Liverpool. She was very concerned about her husband, who was travelling on the storm-tossed ship. One night, when the storm finally began to abate, Mr Wilmot managed to sink into a relaxing sleep on the vessel and he experienced a weird, vivid dream. He dreamt that his wife entered the state-room wearing her nightclothes. When she realised that he was sharing the cabin with his friend, a Mr Tait, she hesitated in her steps. Mr Tait, who was lying in the bunk above her husband's, looked up at the unexpected visitor, who finally decided to come across the cabin to kiss her sleeping husband on the lips. Then she quickly and quietly left the cabin.

It was just after 4am when Mr Wilmot woke from the touching dream. He saw Mr Tait staring down at him from his bunk. Mr Wilmot asked him what the matter was, to which he replied that he was confused because he had just seen a woman enter the cabin and that she had kissed Wilmot as he slept and then left. Wilmot asked his cabin-mate to describe the nocturnal visitant and he unhesitatingly gave a description that fitted his wife to a tee.

When Mr Wilmot eventually arrived home in Liverpool, his wife asked him a curious question, had he been visited by her in the night the week before? Her husband simply nodded and said "Yes", but did not elaborate. Mrs Wilmot then told a strange tale. She explained that one night a week back – at the height of her anxiety – she had felt herself coming out of her body to find him. At four in the morning her consciousness left her bed and soared across the city, across the Mersey and over the Irish Sea. She then traversed the dark heaving waters of the North Atlantic until she came to a steamship. Suddenly, she found herself aboard the vessel. She went down the decks at the stern and came into the state-room. She then described the interior of the state-room in precise detail:

"A man in the upper berth was looking at me, and for a moment I was afraid to go in, but soon I went up to the side of your berth, bent down and kissed and embraced you, then went away."

Mr Wilmot was speechless. This case was investigated by the Society for Psychical Research (SPR) and, after the Wilmots and Mr Tait were interviewed, the SPR researchers recorded the perplexing incident in their chronicles.

The Marie Celeste Connection

Most unsolved mystery buffs are familiar with the basic outline of the story of the *Marie Celeste*. She left New York in November 1872 under the command of Captain Briggs with 1,700 barrels of crude alcohol in her hold, bound for Genoa in Italy. On board were Briggs' wife and two-year-old daughter and a crew of eight men.

Almost a month later, David Moorhouse, captain of a ship called the *Dei Gratia*, caught sight of a speck on the horizon, 500 miles east of the Azores. When he scrutinised it more closely through his telescope, he saw that it was a ship that was sailing erratically. He dispatched a boarding party over to investigate and they found the ship, the *Marie Celeste*, totally deserted. The only lifeboat was missing but, in all other respects, the ship was completely seaworthy.

There was a full six months' supply of food and water on the ship and also the crew's oilskins, boots, pipes and tobacco had all been left behind. It was obvious that everyone on board had left the ship in a tremendous hurry for some unknown reason.

After an extensive search, it was discovered that only the navigation instruments appeared to have been taken.

Further investigation revealed that someone had struck the ship's rail with an axe and, in the cargo hold, one of the barrels had been opened. The captain's sword was found on his bed in his cabin and, on a slate, someone had chalked the words, 'Fanny, my dear wife, Frances M R'.

Captain Moorhouse towed the derelict ship to Gibraltar and, after a lengthy court of enquiry, he was awarded a salvage cheque for the princely sum of £2000 for his troubles.

No one has ever fully solved the mystery of the *Marie Celeste* but quite a few people later came forward, claiming that they were survivors of the sea's most famous mystery. Most of these claimants were either publicity-seekers or just plain conmen, out to make a quick buck. But, curiously, two Liverpool sailors were amongst those who said they had been on board the *Marie Celeste* during her fateful last voyage.

One of these was a 92-year-old cook from Maryland Street named Lawrence Keating. He claimed that he had joined the crew at the last minute when one of the original sailors on the *Marie Celeste* refused to set sail because he believed in the ancient superstition that it was unlucky to embark on a merchant voyage with a woman on board (in this case the captain's wife). Keating's account detailed how the ship ran into a hurricane in the mid-Atlantic, which almost turned the ship on its end. During the storm, the piano on board came loose from its moorings and crushed the captain's wife and the captain was utterly devastated by his terrible loss.

Adamantly refusing to confine his wife's decomposing body into the sea, he placed her in the only lifeboat and towed it by rope, behind the *Marie Celeste*. This action caused deep consternation amongst the crew and somebody eventually severed the rope and a fight resulted. The captain then went on the rampage, wielding an axe and threatening everyone in sight. After killing most of the crew, with the storm still raging, he was washed into the sea. Keating had allegedly survived the whole incident by hiding in the cargo hold. However, no one believed his bizarre story and he died two months after his revelations, so his account could be neither authenticated, nor dismissed.

Another Scouser, William Foyle, a notorious thief and confidence-trickster, literally leapt aboard a ship named the *City of Ragusa* bound for Boston, in 1870. Billy Foyle was an inventive and imaginative conman, who was in the habit of selling fake maps of South African diamond mines to the gullible public. When he arrived in America, he embarked on a further series of frauds and, eventually, when the American authorities began to close in on his illegal, entrepreneurial activities, in order to evade capture, he allegedly stowed away on a brig – the *Marie Celeste*.

Now, Billy Foyle had gained such a well-deserved reputation from telling so many whoppers, that no one attempted to believe his version of the *Marie Celeste* mystery, when he reached Liverpool in 1873. At a waterfront tavern in Paradise Street, he told a motley crew of associates that he had been woken up in the hold of the *Marie Celeste* to the sound of an ominous, deafening rumble. Apparently, it was caused by the alcohol in the barrels, fermenting in the sweltering tropical heat.

He was convinced that an explosion was imminent, so he was forced to break his cover and scramble hurriedly up on deck. To his total bewilderment, there was no one there. All the crew had abandoned ship and were huddled together in the only lifeboat, which was attached to the ship by a long line of around 300 yards. Foyle quickly realised that they had also been frightened of the unstable cargo and had consequently put as much distance between themselves and the ship as possible, by taking refuge in the lifeboat.

Foyle repeatedly pleaded with them to allow him onto the boat, but they refused, so he angrily grabbed an axe and severed the tow rope. The lifeboat carrying the crew drifted off towards the horizon and Foyle fell to his knees and prayed for salvation. Inexplicably, the cargo gradually stabilised and the danger subsided. When Captain Moorhouse, who found the ship, was towing the *Marie Celeste* into the harbour at Gibraltar, he saw Foyle come out on deck. Potentially, he could have ruined the salvage prize, so Moorhouse let him go. This account all ties in with the established facts. At the court of enquiry, witnesses stated that an unaccounted-for crew member left the *Dei Gratia* and set out for England. Mystery solved?

I recently uncovered an article in an old newspaper which may throw some light on the fate of the *Marie Celeste's* crew. On 16 May 1873, the *Daily Albion* of Liverpool reported that fishermen at Baudus, in Asturias, near Madrid, had spotted two rafts floating in the Atlantic coastal waters off the Spanish mainland. One of the rafts had a corpse lashed to its side and was flying an American flag. The second raft carried five decomposing bodies. For some unaccountable reason, the reports were never fully looked into, so we will never know from which ship the dead bodies originated. Could they possibly have been from the *Marie Celeste?*

From Liverpool to Limbo

On 1 March 1854, a ship called the *City of Glasgow* left Liverpool Docks, bound for Delaware Bay on the east coast of America, carrying 480 passengers all of them immigrants, looking for a new life across the Atlantic.

The ship weighed 1,080 tons and was one of the finest vessels of her day. If her twin engines failed, she also had sails to fall back on and carried lifeboats, as well as sufficient provisions to feed all the passengers for a good two months. Despite all this, the ship disappeared without trace in the Irish Sea, after it was seen entering a thick band of peculiar bluish fog. The steamer, *Westmorland*, was in the area at the same time, just in front of the *City of Glasgow*, as was another ship, the *Baldaur*, which was sailing a couple of miles behind, in the wake of the missing ship.

The crews of both these ships were baffled by the *City of Glasgow's* disappearance. Not a single stick of wreckage was ever found and, to this day, the fate of the ship, which had a steel hull, is still a mystery. It is as if the ship, and all 480 people on board, simply vanished into thin air.

There is a strange epilogue to this tale. In 1915, the *UB-64*, a German submarine, was patrolling the same stretch of the Irish Sea, when the captain spotted an outdated steamer through his periscope. According to the captain, as they drew nearer to this ship, they could make out part of the name on the stern, which was partly obscured in mist; it read 'Glasgow'. Seconds later, the antiquated ship seemed to just melt away in the mist.

Angels

There are around nine hundred angels mentioned in the bible, but, interestingly, not one of them is actually described as having wings. The medieval artists added the wings and the halos and the harps, but the bible just says that angels are superior to human beings and act as messengers. They are usually described as human-like, clad in radiant clothes and are often described as being very tall.

American Dream

Throughout history, a number of prominent people have claimed to have met angels. One of these people was George Washington. Washington was a very religious man, who was often mocked because he used to go into the bushes to pray.

During the dark days of the American War of Independence (1775-1783), Washington emerged from his house one day looking very pale. When Anthony Sherman, one of his staff, asked him if he was feeling okay, he told him that he had just had an encounter with an angel. Washington made Sherman swear that he would not tell anyone until after he had died and then proceeded to give an account of how he had been sitting in his study, browsing through his book collection, when a brilliant light exploded throughout the room. He turned around to find that there was an extremely beautiful woman standing before him, dressed in a one-piece silvery blue garment.

"Who let you in?" he asked rather sternly. "I gave strict orders that I am not to be disturbed."

"Son of the Republic, look and learn," she replied, enigmatically and pointed to a ball of mist that was materialising in front of her.

Inside this mist, Washington saw terrifying scenes of warfare. There was a strange flag with an unchristian cross of stars and the faces of black people crying. This has since been interpreted as the American Civil War, which erupted about a century later. Then the mist cleared and Washington saw a futuristic age when North and South America were united under one red blue and green flag. Then the angel faded away. This story is actually mentioned in Sherman's biography, although a lot of historians dismiss Washington's claim as an example of religious mania.

Cloud of Angels

There is a very fine line between angels and beings from outer space. In October 1843, several people in Clwyd, in North Wales, saw what they described as a remarkable cloud passing over St Asaph. An old barrel-maker who was watching this circular-shaped cloud, was amazed to see three human-shaped figures in white drifting down from the sky. The old man rushed into the local inn and alerted a crowd of drinkers at the bar. They followed him out and also witnessed the three figures flying about at treetop level. The same odd-looking cloud and the figures in white, passed over Merseyside and were also seen in south Lancashire, where people reported the figures as being angels, because of the way they flew through the air.

Guardian Angel

In 1985, a Warrington woman and a St Helens man were sitting in their car in the Cheshire countryside, admiring the view, with the woman's Alsatian dog was lying on the back seat. A man emerged from the woods nearby and beckoned them repeatedly to come to him. They thought he might be mentally disturbed, so they tried to ignore him but he persisted. Eventually, accompanied by the Alsatian, they went over to the man and asked him what the matter was.

They were stopped in their tracks by a loud smashing and banging behind them; a runaway tractor had overturned and rolled down a hill and flattened the couple's parked car. If they had still been in the car they would have been crushed to death. Instantly realising that the mysterious stranger had actually saved their lives, they turned towards him but he was nowhere to be seen. He must have heard the tractor hit the car. Indeed, he must have seen it happen. So where was he? The Alsatian ran across to a tree nearby and kept looking up at the branches and wagging its tail, as if it could see someone – but there was nobody there.

Years later, the woman attended a séance at a spiritualist church in Liverpool's Daulby Street. The medium said to her, unprompted, "You've got a guardian angel, you know. There's a man looking over you. He isn't a spirit who has lived, he's some sort of spirit guide. He's close-by now."

Angel at the Roadside

Another case of a guardian angel was in 1966. An elderly man, Frankie Myers, from Sunlight Street, Liverpool was on his way to visit his brother in September Road near Cabbage Hall. As he was crossing Lower Breck Road, a coal wagon came hurtling towards him – the vehiclewas swerving across the road, due to faulty brakes. Old Mr Myers just froze in the middle of the road and closed his eyes, fully expecting to be knocked down, when someone, or something, pushed him out of the path of the wagon, which careered past him out of control.

After he had picked himself up and dusted himself down, he looked around to thank his saviour but there was absolutely no one about. When he later told his parish priest about the incident, the priest said that he had heard of other similar incidents happening on the same stretch of road over the years.

Blue Angel

In 1910, an 14-year-old girl went to stay the night with her grandmother in a house near Roscommon Street in Everton. At around midnight, they both got into bed, but the old lady was unable to settle because her throat was dry, so she asked her granddaughter to go down to the kitchen to fetch her a glass of water. The young girl took a candle and bravely descended the dark staircase.

At the bottom of the third flight of stairs, something was giving off a soft blue glow. As she moved closer, she saw that the light was actually emanating from the phosphorescent image of a woman and she turned on her heels and raced back upstairs to her grandmother and buried herself beneath the blankets. Eventually her grandmother, who was not the nervous type, persuaded her to go back down the stairs with her, to take another look. But, when they reached the foot of the staircase, there was no one there.

"There's no one here, pet. It must have been your imagination," said the old woman. "Come on, let's go back to bed."

"But, she was standing right here, Gran, honest," insisted the girl.

She pointed to a spot on the steps and, at that spot, the grandmother was horrified to see that one of the steps had collapsed and was in a very dangerous condition. The phantom woman in blue had saved the little girl from having a serious accident on the stairs. To her dying day, the woman who had been that little girl, was convinced that her life had been saved by her guardian angel that night.

Seeing Double!

Me and my shadow, walking down the avenue...
Billy Rose

Carbon Copy

We often say, when impossible demands are made of us, that we cannot be in two places at once, as if we are stating the obvious. Yet there have been many recorded instances of the doppelganger – an exact double of a living person that is supposed, by legend, to stalk us all. These phantasms of the living are said to stay out of sight of their worldly counterpart until he or she is approaching death, or experiencing a serious illness; then they usually visit their twin, or even their double's friends. Here is an intriguing report of a doppelganger incident which is alleged to have taken place in Everton in May 1995.

Terry saw his own doppelganger three times and, on each occasion, he was terrified by the experience. When he encountered it the first time he was on a bus up in Walton Road. He glanced out of the window and saw his spitting image, dressed in the very same clothes he was wearing himself that day, coming out of a newsagents, reading a copy of the *Daily Mirror*, Terry's favourite tabloid newspaper.

Terry often visited that particular newsagents shop to purchase his newspapers and magazines and was extremely shaken by the sighting. He stood up on the bus and rushed to the rear window of the vehicle to get a better glimpse of his eerie carbon copy, almost knocking an old lady to the ground in the process.

On the second occasion, Terry walked into his local barber's and took a seat, to wait his turn. The barber glanced round and commented to Terry that his hair had grown very fast. Terry just grinned amicably, without appreciating what he actually meant. When the barber had finished with his customer, he walked over to Terry, eyed his hair with a puzzled look and muttered, "You were only in here last week."

"No, I wasn't," Terry protested, thinking the hairdresser was confusing him with someone else.

"You were. Don't you remember? You were feeling depressed," the barber insisted.

"I never set foot in here last ..." Terry began, when he suddenly remembered the doppelganger incident on the bus.

He related the incident to the barber, who turned white. He started to talk to Terry's mirror image, which is a common idiosyncrasy of many hairdressers.

"You're winding me up," he said.

"Before God, I saw my double," continued Terry, who was a born-again Christian. "Same clothes, same height and build, same face."

"You're giving me the creeps, Tel," the hairdresser shuddered, still addressing his mirror image.

"You said he was depressed, what did you mean?" Terry continued.

"That's just it, You – or he, never said anything, which wasn't like you. You usually can't stop nattering, can you? I presumed you were down in the dumps. Oh, I think you're having me on."

The barber smiled at Terry, expecting him to admit to some hoax, but it was plain that he was genuinely worried.

Later that day, Terry visited a friend who did the Tarot cards and was really into the occult. This 'friend' told Terry that he was being stalked by his doppelganger, which meant that his number was up.

"This is brilliant. I'd love to see it. When you meet your doppelganger and touch it, you both die, like matter touching anti-matter, it's mutual destruction," he added insensitively.

Feeling completely distraught by this stage, Terry told his neighbour about the double and it was she who wrote a letter on his behalf and addressed it to me at Radio Merseyside. I receive a considerable amount of mail from time-wasters, attention seekers and various other cranks so, initially, I concluded that someone in listener-land was playing a prank on me but, eventually, I rang Terry's neighbour and arranged a meeting. Terry was very sincere and asked me to refrain from turning his bizarre predicament into fodder for the media. He did not want his name or address to be given on air, although I assured him he would be able to come on the *Billy Butler Show* without supplying his name.

"Billy and Wally are very understanding in these matters," I told him, "and they wouldn't treat this unusual situation in their usual jokey, sarcastic manner, if they thought it'd upset you."

Alas, Terry refused to come on air. He asked me to tell him frankly if I also thought his number was up. I explained to him that I have read an awful lot of literature on doppelgangers over the years. The myth that they were an omen of impending doom was just an old wives' tale and nothing more and I told him so. I advised him to carry a camera so that he could take a snapshot of his double, just to prove to himself that it was not all in his mind. However, he seemed insulted by the suggestion and testily stated that he did not need to prove that his wraith was real, he just wanted to be rid of it. In the end, I told a psychical researcher in Hunts Cross about the case and he looked into it.

He became like another shadow, tailing Terry everywhere he went. He, too, saw the doppelganger, strolling down Barlow Lane one Sunday morning. The lane was deadly quiet and the researcher cried out to Terry, "There it is. It's coming this way." And so it was. The uncanny figure was walking towards the two men, glancing down at the ground, apparently in a sombre mood. Terry turned and was about to flee, as his nerves got the better of him, but the researcher seized him firmly by the shoulders and held him so that he was forced to face his sinister mirror image.

When the doppelganger was around 50 feet away, it suddenly noticed it's original counterpart. The figure turned and ran, with the researcher running close behind. The doppelganger turned the corner into Westminster Road and when the researcher turned the same corner, seconds later, the double had mysteriously vanished.

It was seen on one more occasion, strolling amongst the milling crowds in Church Street, near the entrance to the C&A clothing store, when Terry was in town, shopping with his girlfriend. He pointed the double out to her and she was astounded to find that all Terry's accounts of his encounters with his doppelganger were true after all. However, she believed there must be a rational explanation – she speculated that perhaps Terry's mother had given birth to twins, who had been separated for some reason. The doppelganger walked up the street and turned a corner with Terry and his girlfriend in hot pursuit. They lost sight of it in the crowds near the Bluecoat Chambers.

Since that day, Terry has never set eyes on his second self, but a fortnight after the grand finale, there was one last calling card from his alter ego. Terry visited Anfield Cemetery in order to place a bouquet of roses on his mother's grave, but was perplexed to find that someone had already placed a similar bouquet there already.

The note attached to the floral tribute read: 'Still miss you loads, Mum. Love, Terry. xxx '

At this Terry snapped. He became paranoid and suspected that his occult-obsessed friend had played a sick joke on him. Later that day he waylaid his friend as he was reading a dusty old tome about the supernatural in his usual haunt – a secondhand bookshop in Mount Pleasant. His friend denied playing any distasteful prank and was quite offended by the suggestion. He even produced a creased rail ticket to prove that he had been staying with his cousin in Wales for the previous three days.

Terry apologized. He was so shaken by his skirmishes with his creepy simulacrum, that he finally moved house and rented a flat near Rodney Street. To date, he has not bumped into his flesh and blood replica. But every time he turns a corner, he wonders if he will see it again.

Home Sweet Home

Our second doppelganger case occurred in the mid-1980s in a house on Church Road, Wavertree, not a stone's throw from Penny Lane. The four-bedroomed house had no history of hauntings or ghostly goings-on, so it was a shock for the Davis family (and their year-old Labrador, Cecil) to watch the phantom of a middle-aged woman walking down their stairs one afternoon. Cecil was so terrified, that he crashed headlong through the bottom pane of glass in the kitchen door in his cowardly retreat from the unwelcome entity. Fortunately, he did not suffer a scratch.

Upon reaching the bottom of the stairs, the ectoplasmic woman seemed to break up into millions of spots before disappearing completely. Mr Davis described how she had dematerialised the way Captain Kirk does on *Star Trek* when they beam him up. He said that her image seemed to break up into a myriad of luminous specks.

The ghost was seen many more times, mostly during the daytime. It strolled across the front garden lawn on one occasion and was seen by the postman, who initially took it to be a real person until it performed its usual uncanny dissolving act.

A year later, Mr Davis had an opportunity to work in Hoylake and decided to put his house on the market and move across the water. Imagine his surprise when he met the first person who came to view it – a woman who was identical to the now-familiar phantom lady. Her face, hairstyle and build, were all identical to the apparition's. The woman gave her name as Mrs O'Rourke. She claimed that she had been born in the Davis's house in the 1930s and had spent most of her teenage life there. Mr Davis was flabbergasted.

Mrs O'Rourke said that she often visited the house in her mind and imagined walking around its interior. When she had seen the for sale sign outside, she just had to take the opportunity to stop by and view the place of her childhood. Mr Davis told her about the ghost that had been haunting the house and suggested that it was perhaps her mother's spectre. She gave a lop-sided grin then calmly said:

"Oh, no, that wasn't mother. It was probably me. You may think I'm mad, but I think I somehow projected my image here during my nostalgic ramblings. People have told me about this type of thing before. When I couldn't make it to Oxford Street Maternity hospital when my daughter was giving birth because I had the flu, two nurses swore they saw me in the ward where my daughter was."

Mr Davis introduced Mrs O'Rourke to the rest of his family and they were amazed at the likeness between their guest and the resident ghost. When Cecil the dog set eyes on Mrs O'Rourke, he fled for cover beneath the stairs and howled. His behaviour seemed to prove that something strange was definitely going on.

Sadly, three months later, Mrs O'Rourke died after a short illness and the Davis family finally sold their house and moved away. As far as I know, the new owners of the house on Church Road have not had any encounters with the phantom lady.

Double Quick

Another doppelganger story, with a Liverpool connection, is mentioned in the July 1991 edition of the *ForteanTimes*, a monthly magazine about strange phenomena which derives its name from the iconoclastic philosopher and student of the unexplained, Charles Fort (1874-1932). In the letters column of the magazine, there is an intriguing account of a doppelganger in the north of Liverpool from Rob Gandy of Bebington, on the Wirral.

"About two years ago (1981), I was driving down County Road in Kirkdale, Liverpool, towards the city centre. The traffic was fairly heavy as people were returning home in the early evening. I pulled up at the Spellow Lane traffic lights which were on red – I was about four cars back from the lights in the outside lane. I noticed a rather plump woman, in a garish outfit, cutting through the stationary cars to cross the road. She walked immediately in front of my car, from left to right, before crossing when there was a gap in the oncoming traffic. With her blonde hair piled up on the top of her head and her striking attire, this middle-aged woman was very remarkable in appearance, arguably for the wrong reasons.

The lights changed and I set off down Walton Road into Kirkdale Road, with the traffic flowing reasonably quickly. I then had to stop at the traffic lights at the junction of Great Homer Street – which are about three-quarters of a mile from Spellow Lane. To my amazement, the same woman cut through the stationary vehicles, immediately in front of my car, from left to right. There was no mistaking her, unless she had a twin sister who was dressed identically. There is no way that I can conceive of how the woman managed to travel from the first position to the second, in what must have been about 90 seconds, given the absence of any transport."

All we can do is hazard a guess and surmise that all the previous accounts outlined in this chapter are examples of the doppelganger. According to psychical researchers, ghosts of the living are the commonest type of apparition. This claim is backed up by a report carried out in November 1994 by the British Journal of Psychiatry, which examined 56 doppelganger episodes that year, including the case of a pilot who saw himself several yards away for a full ten minutes. The report also investigated an intriguing incident concerning a real-looking doppelganger which stalked a retired doctor.

Until scientists can open their minds to the reality of the doppelganger, societies will continue to live in fear of this phenomenon. Perhaps one day we will discover a complex biological mechanism which causes the human body to create a seemingly physical simulacrum of itself. This is not as far-fetched as it seems. Cell multiplication was not discovered until 1844, when the Swiss anatomist and embryologist, Kolliker, astounded the medical world by proving that a human being begins its life as two cells which split up and multiply. Perhaps, when we die, we also split up and produce an intangible etheric body which leaves its earthly replica behind to decay. Maybe in times of illness, or great emotional stress, or in a near death situation, this 'secondary body' is projected from its physical duplicate, or becomes prematurely detached in some way. This theory would make some sense of the doppelganger phenomenon.

Warnings from the Other Side!

According to American psychical researchers, most people receive premonitions in their subconscious minds when they are asleep. Experts in the paranormal now believe that, if you keep a notepad by your bed and jot down an account of each dream as soon as you wake up, you will be surprised at how many of the events portrayed in your dreams, come to pass in reality over a period of weeks and months, or even days. This theory would explain the baffling phenomenon of déjà vu – the strange sensation people sometimes get which makes them feel that they have already been to a place they have not actually visited before, or they know what is going to happen before it occurs. Perhaps you dreamed of being in a particular place months before, but the memory became lost in your subconscious. So keep a dream diary if you want a glimpse of the future – why should it not be ours to see?

A Woman's Intuition

In 1838, a German-born businessman named Johann Adolphus kissed his young wife Louisa goodbye, before leaving his palatial house in Abercromby Square. He stepped into a waiting carriage loaded with luggage and waved one last time to Louisa, who stood tearfully on the front step. The carriage took Mr Adolphus to the docks, where he boarded a steamer bound for Bombay. Johann was an importer of tea and various commodities from India and his stay overseas was likely to last up to six months, sometimes more. These bouts of prolonged absence were not exactly conducive to his marriage to Louisa, who was 25 years younger than 50-year-old Johann.

Two months later, Louisa's elderly maidservant and companion, Mrs Hastings, suffered a stroke and died. Louisa's Aunt, Moira Hennessey thought that a 16-year-old orphan girl she had adopted would make a fine trainee maid. The young girl was Rose Fitzpatrick, a shy but beautiful brunette who spoke with a slight speech impediment. Louisa hired Rose straight away and found her to be a most conscientious and hardworking girl. One of Louisa's faults was her aloofness where servants and maids were concerned, but she felt as if she had known Rose all her life and the two grew extremely close.

One day, Louisa was watching the new maid cleaning the silverware in the drawing room, when Rose suddenly stopped polishing and began to stare into space, as if in an hypnotic trance.

"What is the matter?" Mrs Adolphus asked, but she received no reply.

After blankly staring for a few moments longer, Rose suddenly announced, with a dazed look:

"Mrs Waln has just died ma'am."

"Who is Mrs Waln?" Mrs Adolphus asked, intrigued.

"She was a friend of my guardian, Mrs Hennessey," the young maid explained, with a grave expression.

Nothing more was said until later in the evening, when Moira Hennessey arrived at the house. She unwittingly confirmed Rose's claim; Mrs Hannah Waln, a neighbour of Moira's, had died earlier that day, aged 112. Strangely, she had passed away at the very hour of Rose's bizarre remark. Louisa put the eerie incident down to coincidence, but there were many more unusual episodes concerning the young maid.

One Sunday afternoon, Louisa and Rose were strolling through Abercromby Square on their way to chapel, when a tall man tipped his hat as he walked by. After a few moments, Rose told her employer that the same man had recently written love-letters to the lonely wife, she added that the gentleman's name was Ralph. Mrs Adolphus was outraged by Rose's bizarre suggestion of a romantic attachment, yet she was intrigued at her supernatural knowledge, because she knew that the man's name really was Ralph Foster. He was a business associate of her husband and had been a guest at her home on two occasions, but Ralph had never showed an iota of romantic interest in Louisa, or so she thought.

Strangely, on the following day, Mrs Adolphus received an anonymous letter from someone who professed to be deeply in love with her. Rose was immediately quizzed about her clairvoyant talent, but the maid said she knew nothing about her strange abilities, only that she had possessed them for as long as she could remember.

No further reference was made to the issue for some time, until Louisa's curiosity got the better of her. One quiet evening Mrs Adolphus asked Rose if she could tell her how her husband was keeping, all that way away in Bombay. The maid sat gazing at the hearth, her eyes fixed on the flames. She then made a very controversial claim which shocked Louisa to the marrow. She stated that Johann Adolphus had another wife, a Dutch woman named Julia, who was living with him in India. Mrs Adolphus angrily rejected Rose's scandalous claims at first, but after some months had passed, she ended up travelling to Bombay with a relative to visit her husband, and to also find out whether or not he was a bigamist.

It turned out that he was. Johann had been married to a Julia von Veltheim for four years, leading a double life with a new family in Bombay. On discovering the truth, Louisa ensured that her marriage to him was annulled. Johann remained abroad to avoid imprisonment, while Louisa returned home devastated. She retained Johann's properties in Liverpool and some years later she became engaged to Ralph Foster and in 1842 they married, with Rose as the chief bridesmaid.

Dreams of Murder

On the stormy night of 9 December 1913, a 50-year-old Anfield woman named May Shambrook went to bed just after twelve o'clock. She was exhausted and so, as soon as her head hit the pillow, she was asleep. She fell into an intense slumber, experiencing a pleasant dream about a young man who lived across the road in Windermere Street. The man she dreamt about was 21-year-old George Sumner; in the dream, the young man was smiling at a woman across a room as he brushed the floor with a broom. The woman in the dream was beautiful, she looked to be about 35 to 40 years of age. She was pleasantly smiling back at George as she counted coins on a shop counter of some sort. It seemed that Mrs Shambrook was dreaming about the inside of what looked like a chandlery shop.

As the vivid dream progressed, suddenly George Sumner threw down the broom and his face became contorted with an extreme expression of pure hatred. With a look of evil, he fixed a stern glare on the female counting the coins. The woman's eyes widened in surprise and at this stage of the dream, May had become restless and distressed in her sleep. The dream went on and Sumner suddenly attacked the woman, grabbing at her as he violently ripped off her clothes. During the struggle, he aggressively tore off her blouse and grabbed at her breasts, before pinning her down on the counter. After raping the woman, he picked up a wooden stick of some sort and began to batter his petrified victim, who, half naked, was desperately trying to scramble away. The nightmare was so vivid, May Shambrook could see the blood showering Sumner as he hit the woman. The walls of the shop were stippled in crimson blood.

At this point, Mrs Shambrook woke up sweating, paralysed with anxiety for some time. Distraught, she told her husband about the dream, who reassured her that it had just been a bad nightmare. May Shambrook, still feeling uncomfortable, eventually drifted back to sleep, only to experience another disturbing dream. This time, she could still see the shop of horrors, where she could picture two figures struggling with the corpse of a half-naked woman. The men were doubling the body up and trying to force it into a sack. One of the men was again George Sumner and he was swearing at the corpse because he was having difficulty getting it into the sack. The limp head of the body fell sideways and the disturbed dreamer saw that it was the face of the murdered woman from the shop.

May woke up utterly traumatised. Telling herself to ignore the horrible dream, she lay back, her pulse still racing. Despite trying, she hardly slept again that night.

The next day she told a neighbour about the nightmare which she had had about George Sumner. Her neighbour, Mrs Green, dismissed it as just a nasty nightmare. She had chortled, "George Sumner wouldn't hurt a fly".

On the following day, the local news announced that the manageress of a shop in Old Hall Street had gone missing. It was the same shop where George Sumner worked. The missing woman was 40-year-old Christina Bradfield and she was Sumner's boss.

A day after the disappearance, Miss Bradfield's body was found floating in the Leeds-Liverpool canal, crumpled awkwardly inside a sack. She was found topless, with numerous injuries to her battered head. It also transpired that the poor victim had been raped.

Police put together the facts of the case. After quizzing the shop staff, they called at the house of George Sumner, who was suspiciously nowhere to be seen. His workmate, an 18-year-old named Samuel Elltoft, was interrogated by detectives and broke down. He recalled how his colleague, George Sumner, had been brushing up in the shop as he watched Miss Bradfield counting the day's takings. Suddenly George Sumner had lost his temper and had brutally attacked and raped the manageress, before beating her to death with a wooden baton. The distraught boy emotionally told how Sumner had given him these details and then bullied young Elltoft into disposing of the body, warning him that they would both hang if a body was found. He explained how they had hurriedly put the body in a sack and taken it by cart to the Leeds-Liverpool Canal, where they had dumped it.

George Sumner was finally captured by the police. He had been staying at a lodging house in St James Street. Tried at St George's Hall in February 1914, the brutal man was sentenced to hang. His young workmate, Samuel Elltoft, was found guilty of being an accessory to the horrific incident and was sentenced to four years' hard labour.

When May Shambrook read the details of the murder in the *Liverpool Echo*, she felt unbelievably distraught. A freezing cold shiver ran down her spine as she realised that she had witnessed most of the grisly details in her strange vivid dreams. Tis single instance of prophetic vision was unexplainable and, to her relief, she never encountered such a gruesome nightmare again.

The Bookies' Nightmare

As most people probably know, a premonition is a supernatural warning. These warnings can take the form of dreams, hunches, gut feelings, etc and, of course, people such as psychics just have a knack of knowing whether something good or bad will happen at a future date.

I have had quite a few remarkable letters from BBC Radio Merseyside listeners who have had premonitions. I received one in March 1996 from a Tuebrook woman named Joan, who told me that she had dreamt that a horse wearing the number seven had won the Grand National. She also said that the jockey on this horse wore a red cap. Well, Rough Quest won the National and his horse did wear the number seven and the jockey riding it, M Fitzgerald, did wear a cherry red cap.

Joan claims that, although she is not interested in gambling, she has frequently dreamed which horses would win certain races and her husband has often backed them and won a considerable amount of money as a result. Her husband's nickname for her is the 'the bookies' nightmare'.

Another person who foresaw future winners of horse races at Aintree was John Godley, otherwise know as Lord Kilbracken. In 1958, he dreamt that a horse called Mr What would win the Grand National – a month before the names of the runners were even announced. He later backed Mr What and won over £20,000. He also accurately predicted the racing results of three other race meetings and was given the job of racing correspondent on the Daily Mirror on the strength of it.

A Nightmare Comes True

In the early hours of one morning in 1979, a woman in Netherley named Maureen McAllister suffered a bout of insomnia. She was so restless in her bed that her husband, Jack, was woken up by her fidgeting and asked her what the matter was. Maureen mumbled that she couldn't sleep. Dragging herself out of bed, she went downstairs to the kitchen for a cigarette. As she went to put the kettle on, she heard a sudden noise outside. Entering the dark hall, she pulled the curtain of the small window in the front door aside. What she saw was to haunt her for the rest of her life.

In the moonlight, she witnessed a hearse drive up to the door. This obviously did not make sense, as the time was a quarter to four in the morning. Next to the coffin she could see a distinctive floral tribute that spelt out the word 'mum'. Maureen was unable see the driver of the car, who was just a motionless silhouette.

Doubting what was before her eyes, she ran upstairs to her husband in a state of terror. When she finally awakened him, she pulled him out of the bed and almost pushed him down the stairs.

Jack McAllister sleepily squinted through the window of the front door and he too saw the sinister out-of-hours hearse parked silently in the street. He hurriedly unbolted the door and slid off the security chain, but when the front door was pulled open, the McAllisters saw that there was no hearse there. Jack walked to the front gate and looked both ways up the road, but could see only the parked cars of the people in the street. There was no hearse to be seen.

That morning at five o'clock, Maureen McAllister finally fell asleep. After just a few minutes she suddenly awoke in a cold sweat. She had experienced a terrible nightmare, in which a large building was on fire. She could see a bunch of arms reaching through the bars of a window. Black smoke was pouring through the window and the people inside were screaming and coughing, they were obviously the victims of a fire. Maureen was restless for the remainder of the night, uncomfortably troubled by the strange occurrences disturbing her sleep.

"What a night!" she sleepily reflected over breakfast.

Later on, when her husband went to work, she was wondering about the significance of the funeral hearse with the chilling flowery message. She also remembered the distressing nightmare about the people in the fire.

Moments later the telephone rang. It was Maureen's friend in Manchester asking if she wanted to stay over with her next week. Maureen decided she would love to go and so made travel arrangements that day. In her excitement, she put the unusual events of the previous night to the back of her mind. However, on the day on which she was supposed to visit, Jack broke his arm on a building site. Maureen therefore chose to stay and look after him, despite his attempts to urge her to have a well deserved break with her friend in Manchester.

Shockingly, the very next day, Maureen's friend died in a tragic blaze at Woolworths in Manchester, along with eleven other victims. It seemed that most of the victims of the blaze were overcome with the toxic fumes given off by the fire in the upholstery section. Maureen was utterly distraught, whenever she had been to stay with her friend in the past, they had always paid a visit to Woolworths. Her recollections of that awful sleepless night, only weeks earlier, came to her mind and made her shudder. Maureen knew that had she gone to stay with her friend, she too would have perished in that dreadful blaze.

Don't Go!

In 1912, a Liverpool woman named Mary Richardson, of Boaler Street, off West Derby Road, experienced three nightmares in succession one night, involving an enormous ship sinking beneath the waves. She later saw a newspaper picture of a ship which was exactly like the one in her dreams: it was the *Titanic*, which was about to make its fateful maiden voyage from Southampton to New York. To make matters worse, Mrs Richardson's cousin, a Mr Reginald Butler, wrote to her saying that he had just booked a passage on the maiden voyage of the *Titanic*.

Mrs Richardson wrote back, urging her cousin not to undertake the voyage, but he went ahead anyway and was one of the 1,513 people who went down with the liner in the Atlantic a week later and drowned. Incidentally, Adolf Hitler's half brother, Alois Hitler, had begged Adolf to emigrate to America and had pleaded with him to board the *Titanic* at Cherbourg, but Hitler had a phobia of ships and decided not to go on the liner.

Playing with Fire

I received a letter from a woman in the Dingle who told me a sad tale about a friend she had had when she was a little girl. This girl – let's call her Susan – used to play doctors and nurses and other games in which she pretended that she was an adult. Nothing unusual in that you might say but, whenever Susan played such games, she would invariably chant the same phrase, "My house catches fire and I run upstairs – and I hide in the wardrobe. But I die in the fire".

Many years later, when she had grown up, she died in the very same circumstances which she had repeatedly acted out when she was a child. She was trapped in a blaze in the bedroom of her house and hid in a wardrobe to escape the smoke. Passersby called the fire brigade but she died before the firemen could rescue her.

Danger! Men at Work!

In 1955, a Liverpool man named Terry Phillips was working on a building site down in Lambeth in London. He was walking to the building site one dark winter's morning, when he passed a man wearing black, funereal clothes, standing in a doorway. This man had a terribly disfigured face – Terry Phillips described it as looking like, "Lon Chaney in the *Phantom of the Opera*", and he ran off towards the building site in fright.

A few days later, he was just finishing work and was about to enter the cradle which transported the workers down from the top of the building – when he came face to face with the man with the disfigured face standing in the cradle, just behind the cradle operator. Mr Phillips immediately turned on his heels and ran down the building's 15 flights of steps, rather than stay in the cradle.

On his way down, he heard a tremendous crash. The cable to the cradle had snapped, allowing it to crash down the shaft, killing the cradle operator instantly as it hit the ground. The man with the disfigured face was nowhere to be seen. Terry Phillips firmly believed that the strange figure had been some kind of omen of danger, which had saved his life.

Lucky Escape

I received another interesting letter about a premonition from Maureen, of Prestatyn in North Wales, who was originally from Liverpool. She wrote that, during World War Two, her family, who lived in the south end of the city, had lost its home in the air-raids but, luckily, had subsequently found a new house to rent. When they were inspecting this new house, her mother found that the bedroom door would not open, no matter how hard they pushed and pulled. She had a funny feeling about this and had declared, "That's it! We're not moving to this place!" and she moved the family into her parents' house instead.

That night, the house with the troublesome bedroom door was blasted to pieces when a bomb fell directly on it in the May Blitz.

Sinister Sketches

In the 1970s, firefighters fought a fierce blaze which had broken out in a Liverpool house. A grandfather and his three grandchildren perished in the fire and when investigators sifted through the charred debris to determine the cause of the blaze, they uncovered a small drawing book which had escaped the flames virtually intact. On the pages of this book, someone, possibly the old man, had made a series of sketches featuring three small coffins and a large one, together with a drawing of a burning house. Were these macabre doodles evidence of a premonition that he may have had, of the fatal fire, or of something even more sinister?

Cries for Help

In another instance, a woman was enjoying watching a film at her local cinema one afternoon in the 1980s. Her husband had gone off for the afternoon to Sheffield, to watch Liverpool play Sheffield Wednesday at Hillsborough. Suddenly she was overwhelmed by a horrible feeling of being crushed and suffocated.

As she pulled at her clothes and gasped for air, she heard the anguished cries of her son and husband calling out to her and she intuitively knew that something terrible had happened to them. She was later to receive the tragic news that they had both perished in the Hillsborough disaster and that they had died at the precise time that she had heard their voices calling out to her in the cinema.

You Are Mine Now!

Sometimes, a premonition can be transmitted via the telephone, as in the following case. In the late 1970s, a Liverpool businessman named Barry was checking calls on his new telephone answering machine, when he heard a sinister, high-pitched voice uttering a stark warning message. He initially thought it was someone playing a silly but rather nasty prank, because the voice sounded like Spike Milligan doing his Goon impression.

"Your plane is going to crash," warned the voiced.

Barry naturally told his wife about the warning message and, when she listened to it, she took it very seriously and immediately encouraged him to cancel the holiday flight which they had booked. He was very reluctant to heed her advice and argued that it was ridiculous to cancel a much-needed holiday, on the strength of one crank telephone call. But Barry's wife was adamant about her strong conviction that the warning was from the 'other side' and she finally managed to dissuade her husband from taking the holiday.

A week later, the plane that would have taken them to Tenerife, crashed into a mountainside, killing all the passengers on board. Barry and his wife shivered with a mixture of horror and relief, as they watched the television reports of the air disaster on ITN's lunchtime news. They had missed their holiday, but at least they were alive!

Years later, the couple were at a party one evening, when some of the guests started messing about with a ouija board. They casually wandered over to watch the proceedings when, without warning, a message addressed to Barry came through saying: "I saved you from the crash, so you are mine now!" He turned very pale as the message sank in, because he and his wife had never told anyone about the warning on the answering machine, which convinced them that this new message must have some authenticity.

The Harlow Street Gypsy

The Romany people possess legendary powers of precognition and I once received an interesting telephone call at Radio Merseyside about the so-called, Harlow Street Gypsy. An elderly lady, Mrs Eleanor Cook, told me that her mother, who lived in Harlow Street in the Dingle in the 1930s, had employed a maid named Virginia, who was of Romany descent. Virginia predicted that Eleanor would marry twice during her lifetime – firstly to a red-haired man who would never reach the age of 40 and secondly to a man with a drooping moustache. Eleanor subsequently married red-haired Charles Wright, who died suddenly, just a few days after his 39th birthday. The Romany's second prophecy also came true, when she married George Cook, who wore a distinctive droopy moustache, two years later.

Virginia, who was still employed by Eleanor at the time of her second marriage, warned her new husband to avoid people bearing the names of Teddy or Peggy. George was something of a sceptic and considered this warning to be completely absurd. But, until a year later, when a Scottish couple moved into the house next door to the Cooks. When George learned that their names were Edward and Peggy, he thought that it was nothing more than an amusing coincidence and happily accepted an invitation from them to attend their house-warming party.

An hour after sitting down at the table during the party, Mr Cook suddenly dropped his knife and fork and grabbed the edge of the table, obviously in severe pain. He asked to be excused, doubled up with excruciating stomach cramps. He assured his wife that he would be fine once he had had a lie down, saying that it was probably a bit of indigestion and he urged her to stay at the party, at least until she had finished her meal.

Later that evening, Mrs Cook, accompanied by Virginia, who had also been to the party, returned home and was horrified to discover a trail of blood leading across the hall and up the stairs. The trail led to the bedroom, where she found the body of Mr Cook, lying in a pool of blood. He had bled to death from a burst ulcer in his stomach.

One day, some time after her husband's death, the subject in Mrs Cook's household turned to religion and the gypsy woman foretold that the Catholic population in the city would one day have an enormous round church built with 16 spires on the top. Mrs Cook and two other people present ridiculed the prediction, but Virginia may well have been referring to the Metropolitan Cathedral, which has around 16 spires, shaped like the crown of thorns. The Harlow Street Gypsy also predicted that the River Mersey would one day turn black – perhaps she had foreseen some future pollution incident, of which there have been several.

You Only Live Twice!

I am today, I am yesterday, I am tomorrow.
As I pass through recurrent births
I am ever young and vigorous,

Egyptian Book of the Dead

The concept of reincarnation is a fascinating one, which has intrigued mankind for thousands of years. The possibility that the soul of an individual surviving death can be reborn in a new body, is a very attractive idea, but is there any real proof of reincarnation? Here are several instances from the north west of the UK.

Take Me Back

Some people believe that it is possible to revisit their former lives through hypnotism. Several years ago, Liverpool hypnotist, Joe Keeton, hypnotized a Liverpool housewife named Ann Dowling and regressed her back over a hundred years. He asked her where she was and she replied that she was in Liverpool in 1850, where she was living in a slum as a poor orphan by the name of Sarah Williams.

Keeton asked her what was happening in Liverpool at the time and she said that She was in a crowd outside the Philharmonic Hall, where there was a great deal of excitement because a foreign singer was coming to visit. When questioned about the singer, Mrs Dowling said that the artiste's name had something to do with a bird. Research later revealed that, in August 1850, a Swedish singer named Jenny Lind had visited the old Philharmonic Hall and she was nicknamed, 'the Swedish Nightingale'.

Graveyard Home

Here is another bizarre story in which hypnotherapy helped to uncover someone's previous existence as a ghost.

In the 1980s, a Bebington lorry driver was driving past a cemetery near Newton-le-Willows, when he experienced the sensation of déjà vu – the strong conviction that he had been in the area before. He passed the same cemetery again a few months later and was overcome by the same uncanny feeling; everything looked familiar but he had never lived in the area. He was so perturbed by the experience, that he told his friend about it and he urged him to visit a qualified hypnotherapist. When the lorry driver was put into an hypnotic trance, he apparently remembered being a ghost at the Newton-le-Willows churchyard.

He gave details of how he used to float up out of his grave and wander about the graveyard and of how it always felt as if he was in a dream. He recalled that some people could see him but they invariably ran away and he felt very lonely and isolated. After the hypnotherapy session, he returned to the cemetery and identified what he believed to have been his grave. The engraving on the marble headstone stated that the person had died in August 1940: the very same month in which the man had been born.

The Victim Returns

I uncovered this bizarre report while trawling through the newspaper archives. The report stated that in 1882, a woman from Maghull named Mrs Richardson took her 7-year-old daughter, Geraldine, to Liverpool on a shopping trip. Mrs Richardson was walking down an alleyway near Sweeting Street, off Dale Street, when her daughter cried out and pointed at a man who was buying flowers. Mrs Richardson asked her daughter what the matter was and Geraldine bluntly stated, "Mother, that man attacked me."

Mrs Richardson was puzzled by her daughter's remark, because she knew Geraldine had never been to the city before. Anyway, just then, the individual whom the girl had pointed out threw down the flowers which he had just bought and ran off.

Apparently, Geraldine went on to then tell her mother that she believed that she had been born before and that in her last life, the man buying the flowers had raped her and stabbed her to death.

Interestingly, later that same week, a man named George Millstead was found hanged near Runcorn. He left a suicide note in which he confessed to the rape and murder of two women in Preston. In the note, he described how he had been driven to suicide after encountering a girl in Liverpool who bore an uncanny resemblance to his last murder victim. He never named the victim, but said that he had committed the crime seven years previously in 1875, the year Geraldine Richardson had been born. This poses the obvious question: was Geraldine Richardson the reincarnation of a woman who had been murdered seven years earlier? It would be poetic justice if it was true; the victim returning from the grave to exact revenge…

Blind Sight

One of the more well-documented accounts that has come to my attention, which seems to prove reincarnation, is the case of a Warrington man who was born blind. Mr James had been totally blind from birth but, nevertheless, had experienced recurrent dreams in which he could distinctly picture a woman's face. When he was hypnotized, he described the face as having rosy red cheeks and blonde hair and claimed that it belonged to his wife. He then went on to describe, in detail, her sparkling jewellery and the stunning sunset visible through a window behind her in his vision. A person who was born blind would be unable to provide such a strongly visual description, suggesting that his persona under hypnosis must have been sighted and therefore from a previous life.

To Hell and Back

In 1977, a pub landlord in Morecambe kept experiencing vivid recurrent dreams about being a highwayman. In the dreams he used to look in a mirror and see himself sporting a three-cornered hat and a black velvet mask of the Lone Ranger type. He always made a point of recounting these dreams to his wife and she eventually became so exasperated by them, that she hired a hypnotist to visit the pub to look into her husband's strange dreams. Having put the landlord into a trance, the hypnotist then asked him about the identity of the man in the mask.

He revealed that his name was Edward Higgins and began talking in a quaint, rural accent. He claimed that he was a gentleman by day who visited church regularly every Sunday but, after dark, he confessed that he was a callous highwayman, holding up stagecoaches all over Cheshire. After three hours of being in a trance, the landlord started screaming that he had been caught. He later turned a deathly pale and said that his captors were going to hang him. At this point, the landlord's wife became seriously concerned for her husband's well-being and urged the hypnotist to wake him up but he simply reassured her that he would be fine.

Suddenly, the pub landlord let out a blood-curdling scream and then fell completely silent. The hypnotist gently asked him where he was and he replied, "I'm in hell. I can see so many faces around me. All bad people". Then the hypnotist woke him up.

It has since been established that there really was a highwayman named Edward Higgins who operated near Knutsford in 1752. By all accounts he was a Jekyll and Hyde character; a gentleman by day and a highwayman by night, until he was finally lynched for his misdeeds.

Pigtailed Messiah

In the 1950s, a Cheshire man named Alfred Moberley was put into an hypnotic trance, during which he claimed to be was Pontius Pilate's gatekeeper. When the hypnotist asked him to describe what was going on at the time, Moberley described how a man named Yeshua was causing trouble by preaching against the authorities.

"Who is Yeshua?" the hypnotist prompted.

"The one who says he is the Messiah," replied Moberley calmly.

"Can you describe him to me?"

"Very tall with a swarthy complexion and a long pigtail," he answered, without hesitation.

Twenty years later, historians discovered that the Jews of Pilate's period wore their long hair as a pigtail and they also found a reference to a 'teacher of righteousness', named Yeshua among the Dead Sea Scrolls.

Ironically, Alfred Moberley had been an atheist throughout his adult life.

A Knock on the Head

In the next case, the subject seems to make a connection with a former incarnation after a knock on the head.

There used to be an overalls warehouse called the Lybro which stood near Mount Vernon in Paddington. In the 1960s, there was an alleged case of xenolalia at the warehouse, which is speaking in a foreign language after suffering shock or concussion. A man named Freddie Worth was unloading a lorry when his workmate accidentally dropped a heavy typewriter directly onto his head.

Worth immediately slumped to the floor and, as his mate went to help him up, he shouted, "Dummkopf" in a weird harsh accent. For over an hour, Worth paced about, ranting on in German, which was odd to say the least, because he could not speak one word of the language. He eyed his colleagues strangely, as if he could not quite recognise them.

Realising that he must be suffering from some form of concussion, he was taken to see a doctor at North View about an hour later. But, by the time that he saw the doctor, the normal Freddie Worth had returned but he was as confused as everyone else when he was told about his bizarre behaviour. Are such cases evidence of former lives, lived in a foreign country?

Faithful Friend

In the 1960s, an Ormskirk widow was startled out of her sleep one night by a black Labrador dog howling in her garden. She opened the window and shouted at it to go away, but it refused to budge. Observing that the young dog had no collar, and being an animal lover, she decided to adopt it. However, as soon as she let the dog into the house, it began acting strangely. It bounded into the living room and made itself comfortable on what had been her late husband's armchair. Naturally, this upset her and she began to have second thoughts about giving the animal a home.

She shouted at the dog and shooed it back out into the garden, upon which it flew over to a rose bush and started pulling and chewing at it. By shaking its head vigorously from side to side, it was able to break off one of the stems and soon returned with a single rose in its mouth. It dropped the rose at the woman's feet and whined pitifully. She immediately recalled how her husband used to cut a single rose stem and give it to her each year as a touching romantic gesture.

On another occasion, the dog started whining and poking its nose into a stack of old LPs belonging to the widow's late husband and eventually it managed to isolate one of them and pull it out. As soon as she put on the Mantovani record – who had been a favourite of her husband's – the dog began to wag its tail gleefully and then curled itself up in the armchair. The woman watched all these events and thought she was going mad.

Some time later, two young boys turned up at the widow's house, accompanied by their mother. They insisted that the Labrador was actually their dog and they had come to reclaim it. The widow was devastated when the boys, without further ado, grabbed the dog and put a collar and lead on it. The dog plainly did not want to leave and had to be dragged forcibly down the path. The widow never saw the dog again but she firmly believed that it had been the reincarnation of her dead husband.

Plane Phobia

Many people now think that reincarnation is a possible explanation of why people have irrational phobias. For example, a woman in St Helens who had a phobia of ships was regressed and revealed that she had died on board the *Lusitania*.

In a book called *The Children that Time Forgot*, by Mary and Peter Harrison, there is an intriguing case of a Blackpool boy who was terrified of aeroplanes. Whenever he caught sight of one in the sky, or even heard the distant drone of a jet engine, he would drop to the floor and do a commando crawl under the nearest table. The basis of his phobia, and also his strange reaction on encountering a plane, were both explained when he was hypnotized. Under hypnosis, he claimed that he had been an

American infantryman involved in jungle warfare, who had been killed when a plane dived down and shot at him.

The Other Mum

Occasionally, people can consciously connect with their previous incarnations, without any external help. Here is one such example from my own experience, in which a young child suddenly began referring to a former life.

Many years ago, my mother's friend presented her four-year-old son with two large, chocolate, Easter eggs one Easter Sunday morning, when he came down for breakfast and was startled by her son's reaction.

"Thanks Mum," he said. "You're better than my other mum, she never got me any Easter eggs."

When his puzzled mother quizzed him about this 'other mum', he told her in a matter-of-fact voice, that he had lived in another family before he was born, but that he must have died as a child, because he remembered that everything just 'went black' one day. As the boy got older, he remembered less and less about his previous existence and, today, he is unable to recall any memories of a former life.

Vampire Tales

The myth of the vampire is a very old one, dating back to ancient Egypt and Greece. Today, in our well-lit sprawling cities, there is no place for such a legend, except in horror films and the books of the American fantasy novelist, Anne Rice. Vampires are just figments of the imagination, the bogey-men of gullible rural peasants who lived in a bygone superstitious age. Or that is what commonsense leads us to believe – but even in modern times, Dracula-like beings continue to be reported.

No Resting Place

Shortly before midnight on 8 June 1993, over a thousand people turned up at a cemetery in Pisco, Peru, in the hope of witnessing the resurrection of an alleged vampire by the name of Sarah Ellen Roberts. Local historians and officials from the British Embassy, had recently been shocked to learn that the corpse of Mrs Roberts had been brought to Pisco from Blackburn, England, by her husband, John Roberts, in 1913, because the British authorities refused to let him bury his wife in England, as they believed her to be a vampire.

Mr Roberts dismissed the refusal as an absurdity, but subsequently bought a lead-lined coffin for his deceased wife and allegedly roamed the world for four years, seeking out a country that would allow him to bury her. Finally, he arrived in Peru, where he was allowed to inter his wife at Pisco for the sum of five pounds. Shortly after the ad hoc burial service, Mr Roberts boarded a ship for England and was never heard of again.

Then the news from England reached Pisco – Sarah Ellen Roberts had been bound in chains and shut up in the lead-lined coffin after being found guilty of witchcraft, murder and vampirism. Just before the lid of the coffin was screwed down, the Lancashire witch had screamed out that she would return from the grave to seek vengeance.

The Peruvian peasants in the town trembled at the news. Eighty years later in June 1993, people visiting a grave in the Pisco cemetery were terrified when they witnessed a large crack appearing in the headstone of the Blackburn woman's grave. That night, over a thousand excitement-seekers and occultists descended on the graveyard, when the word went round that the vampire would rise from her grave at midnight. Hundreds of local women left the town in order to prevent the vampire from being reincarnated in their new-born children and cloves of garlic and crucifixes festooned the front doors of almost every house in the region.

When midnight arrived, the vampire mania reached its peak and police had to be called in to control the hysterical crowds. Shots were fired into the air and slowly the people dispersed. A small group of local witch doctors were apparently allowed to stay at the controversial graveside, where they splashed the cracked headstone with holy water and sprinkled white rose petals all around the grave. The English vampire did not rise up and the witch doctors later celebrated their success at laying the undead woman to rest.

Such superstitious mumbo jumbo is excusable in a remote Peruvian town, but there have also been a number of vampire alerts in the bustling metropolis of London.

45

Unwilling Blood Donors

The first scare occurred in the spring of 1922, when an enormous, black, bat-like creature with a wing span of at least six feet, was seen flying around West Drayton Church during the night of a full moon. Several terrified witnesses watched the creature dive into the churchyard, where it flitted about the tombs. When it was chased by two policemen, the creature let out a loud, blood-curdling screech, flapping its huge wings and soared skywards. An old man who claimed that he had seen the giant bat 25 years previously, maintained that it was the spirit of a vampire who had murdered a woman, in order to drink her blood, in Harmondsworth in the 1890s. Not surprisingly, no one took the old man's tale too seriously.

Later that month, on the morning of 16 April, at around 6am, an office clerk on his way to work, was walking down Coventry Street in London's West End. As he strolled into a turning off the street, something invisible to his eyes seized him and pierced his neck. The man felt blood being drawn from his artery, then fell to the pavement, unconscious. He woke up later in Charing Cross Hospital and told what he could remember of his unusual tale. The surgeons who quizzed him concluded that someone must have stabbed him with a thin tube, but the victim disagreed; he was absolutely certain that no one had been close enough to deliver such a thrust.

Two and a half hours later, something incredible happened, which still defies explanation; a second man was brought into the same hospital. He, too, was bleeding profusely from the lower neck and, when he regained consciousness, he also told how he had been walking down Coventry Street, when something intangible had attacked him on the very same corner where the office worker had been struck down.

Later that evening, a third victim of the invisible assailant was admitted to the hospital. The doctors at Charing Cross were absolutely dumbfounded when the police told them that the latest victim had been stabbed at precisely the same spot as the two other casualties – at a turning off Coventry Street. An investigation into the bizarre crimes was launched, as rumours of a vampire at large in London, swept the capital.

The newshounds of Fleet Street pricked up their ears up at the rumours. The *Daily Express* reported the sinister Coventry Street assaults and asked the police if they had any theories on the strange crimes. A police spokesman reluctantly admitted that the injuries sustained by the three men at Coventry Street defied rational explanation and there had been no headway in finding the bloodthirsty attacker. With his tongue placed firmly in his cheek, a reporter asked the spokesman if the police had considered the theory of the Coventry Street attacker being a vampire. The spokesman just chortled nervously and brought the interview to an abrupt end.

Another rumour swept the city; the Coventry Street vampire had been cornered by the police and killed by a professional vampire hunter, who had been drafted in especially for the job. Furthermore, the bloodsucker had been secretly interred with a wooden stake through its heart, in a deep vault up in Highgate Cemetery. The rumour was traced to a pub in Covent Garden, where an off-duty policeman told a landlord of his part in the vampire hunt that had stretched across London.

Face at the Window

Another vampire was said to be at large in England's picturesque Lake District in 1900. In January of that year, a Captain Edward Fisher left Croglin Grange – a bleak, granite-brick farmhouse in Cumbria – and headed south to Guildford, where he had purchased a new residence for business purposes. The new residents of Croglin Grange were two brothers and their sister, who had jumped at the opportunity of taking up the seven year lease on the secluded property. The trio were popular with the neighbours and seemed to be settling well into their new home. But in the first summer at Croglin Grange, which was infernally hot, the sister found it difficult to get to sleep at night. She would lie in her stifling bedroom, gazing out at the moonlit nightscape beyond the windows.

One night she had opened her bedroom window to try and get some air and was staring out into the darkness when she suddenly noticed the silhouette of a lanky, bony figure, darting across the moonlit lawn outside. Within seconds, the agile, sinister-looking stranger was scaling the wall beneath her, so she slammed the window shut and fastened its catch. Almost paralysed with fear, she stumbled away from the window as she listened to the figure scrambling up the wall. She sat on the end of her bed, trying to shout out to her brothers, but found she could scarcely muster anything louders than a whisper.

Then the figure was at the window. At this close range she could see that it was grotesque. The face was yellowed and shrivelled and the eyes were almost black in their huge, circular sockets. The nose was long and aquiline and the mouth, which was unusually large, showed a set of pointed, gruesome-looking teeth. The creature's bony finger scratched at the window as it picked away at the lead lining of one of the panes. The pane rattled in its frame, then fell inwards, allowing the ghoul to reach in and undo the catch. It quickly managed to leap through the window and bolt across the room towards its terrified prey, who had now collapsed on the bed in sheer terror.

The skeletal freak seized the shaking woman by her hair and held her still, as it bit into her neck with its revolting fangs. In this life-threatening situation, the woman somehow managed to overcome her paralysis to let out a scream which brought her brothers racing into her room. They were just in time to catch a glimpse of the nimble intruder leaping out of the bedroom, through the window. They dashed downstairs, unbolted the door and pursued the ghastly assailant across the lawn and over the neighbouring churchyard wall, where they lost sight of him. The brothers stood staring into the darkness for a while, then returned to attend to their sister. When they saw the crimson fang marks on her neck, they knew that no ordinary intruder had been in her bedroom, but they could not bring themselves to believe that the assailant had been a vampire.

One night in the following March, the creature returned to Croglin Grange during a severe gale. As the winds tore across the barren landscape outside, the bony finger was once again at work, removing a pane from the woman's bedroom window, but this time the howl of the gales swamped the sound of the scratching finger. The woman eventually awoke when the vampire was actually leaning over her. His cold and clammy hand grabbed her neck and she screamed in terror. The two brothers burst into the room, this time armed with pistols. The vampire immediately abandoned its prey and instead attacked the brothers, but one of them opened fire, blasting the bloodthirsty stalker in the thigh.

Apparently unaffected by the gunshot, the Cumbrian vampire spun round and literally dived through the open window. The chase was on again, but this time the brothers saw where the creature went to ground – in an old family vault in a corner of the churchyard. The brothers alerted the local villagers and, on the following morning, over 70 people gathered around the family vault that was said to be the vampire's lair. The brothers and three of the villagers lifted the large sandstone slab of the vault and peered into the darkness beneath. A torch was lit, allowing the crowd to behold the disturbing scene within its murky depths.

Inside were four broken coffins and the remains of their mutilated corpses. A fifth coffin, in the corner, was still intact. The crowd gasped and drew back in revulsion as the brothers lifted the lid of this coffin, to reveal the same hideous creature which had twice attacked their sister at Croglin Grange. The corpse even bore the recent marks of the pistol shot in its thigh. One of the villagers stepped forward and told the brothers that he, too, had seen this same creature of the night, attacking livestock in one of the local fields and he advised that the only way to destroy a vampire was with fire. So he and the brothers took the revolting creature out into the churchyard and, after they had gathered enough wood, the vampire was burned on a huge bonfire.

Lodge Lane Vampire

There have also been sporadic reports of vampires on the loose in Liverpool. In February 1983, a young single mother, living in a bedsit in Lodge Lane with her eight-month-old baby, had the constant feeling that she was being watched. She was not the superstitious or paranoid type, but from the day that she moved into the bedsit, she had experienced the horrible sensation of being observed by someone or something next door, especially at night.

In the end, the edgy electric atmosphere in the bedsit became so intense, that the woman went to Wavertree Road Police Station and told the rather bemused constable about the unpleasant feeling of being watched in the spooky flat. The policeman shook his head and said that he was sorry, but there was nothing he could do. The girl began to sob and she hysterically begged him to send an officer round to investigate the flat adjacent to her bedsit because she felt as if the place was radiating evil. To placate her, he promised to send someone around to look into the matter.

That night, at 10pm, the young woman was watching the *News At Ten*, trying to take her mind off her predicament, when some loud thumps from next door nearly made her jump out of her skin. She looked nervously out of the window and saw, to her relief, that there was a police car parked down below in the street. The police must have responded to her plea and were inspecting the next door flat – hence the banging noises. She put her ear to the wall and could hear the strains of a policeman's radio blurting out.

The police later revealed to her what they had discovered in the flat and the revelation resulted in the girl packing her bags at once. The previous occupier had painted all of the walls black and dotted them with mysterious pentagrams and other occult symbols. In the middle of the floor there was an old coffin, which appeared to be at least a hundred years old.

It had probably been stolen from a tomb in a local graveyard, but it was now empty and there were no traces of the corpse it had once contained. The nameplate was too rusted to be decipherable. Next to the coffin was a mysterious book entitled *The Book of Shadows* and next to it was an empty milk bottle – which contained a small amount of clotted human blood.

No one in the street could remember who the occupier of that flat was and he, or she, never returned, but even the hard-boiled, streetwise policemen claimed that they had experienced an icy chill in the flat. The young mother left that night and went to stay with her auntie on the Wirral.

Grave-Robbing Ghouls

The Lodge Lane Vampire may well have even been a member of the band of ghouls who feature in the following story, which took place in the 1960s. In the autumn of 1967, workmen found an empty coffin in a vacant ground-floor flat in Gambier Terrace, just opposite the Anglican Cathedral. That same week, the police issued a sinister warning to all schools in the city, telling all children to avoid the area around St James' Cemetery, as some strange people and unusual events were going on there. The police had become concerned when they saw three children near Percy Street playing football with a human skull, which they had found while taking a shortcut across St James' Cemetery.

The police invaded the graveyard and found evidence of desecration. Several tombs had been opened and, in one of them, they were shocked and saddened to find a ten-year-old, red-haired girl sitting bolt upright in her lead-lined coffin. She was perfectly preserved and looked as if she was sleeping, but she was almost a century old. Her jewellery had gone and pieces of her hair had been chopped off, presumably by the grave-robbing ghouls, to use as a black magic talisman. The corpse was carefully laid back in position in the coffin, which was then resealed and the wall of the tomb bricked up.

Three weeks later, several residents in the area around the Anglican Cathedral tipped off the police when they saw three, sinister-looking, caped figures in black, roaming the cemetery. The police gave chase, but the three men were never caught and one seemed to possess extraordinary athletic skill during the nocturnal pursuit; he jumped high over a gravestone with startling agility and somehow managed to escape from the long arm of the law by bending the wrought iron railings and slipping through the gap. He sped off into the darkness towards Duke Street and evaded capture.

One month later, a prostitute was crossing Hope Street, near the cathedral, at 3am, when a grotesque-looking man in black, with a pallid face, tried to pull her into the shrubbery on nearby wasteland. Like many women in her profession, she was perfectly able to defend herself and let out a shrill scream, then punched her fiendish assailant in the face and he ran off into the darkness. The victim later described her attacker's face by saying that it looked as if he had been hit with a bag of flour.

The Mysterious Abductors

In 1880, William Dean, a young Liverpool teacher, applied for the post of deputy headmaster at a school in West Ham. He was given the job but, during his first term, he noticed that the number of pupils in his class was dwindling rapidly as the weeks went by. He was shocked to learn from two Scotland Yard detectives investigating the disappearances, that a mysterious couple were abducting his pupils, together with other children in the area.

One day, Mr Dean was on playground duty when he caught sight of Eliza Carter, one of the missing school children, staring at him through the school railings. He was anxious not to alarm her, so he walked quietly over to the railings and gently invited her to come back into the school. But Eliza just solemnly shook her head and looked nervously about her.

"I can't, they won't let me," she said, under her breath.

Exactly who 'they' were, was never established, because Eliza then turned and walked quickly away and, by the time Mr Dean had found another teacher to supervise the children in the yard and had set off to look for her, she was nowhere to be seen.

Over 40 children shared Eliza Carter's fate and many of them were last seen talking to a man and a woman. Scotland Yard described the disappearances as 'baffling and sinister' and failed to throw any light on the mystery.

Black Vortex

On 9 December 1873, a Leeds man, Thomas Cumpston, and his Liverpool-born wife, Ann, booked into the Victoria Hotel in Bristol and were promptly given a room. At four o'clock in the morning, the Cumpstons were startled out of their sleep by a howling sound. Mr Cumpston jumped out of bed to see what was happening and, as he lowered his bare feet onto the floor, he started sinking into it. Looking down in alarm, he saw a circular black hole, with a swirling mist inside it and there were loud screeching voices coming from its depths. Mrs Cumpston screamed and leaned over to pull her husband away from the edge of the black vortex. The terrified couple stood on the bed, clinging to each other in fear and disbelief. When Mrs Cumpston had screamed into the vortex, her cries were thrown back at her like an echo.

Mr Cumpston leaned across to the window and flung it open and he and his wife scrambled out onto the ledge and dropped the twelve feet to the ground without stopping to think about the consequences. They ran all the way to the police station in their night clothes and blurted out their story to the desk sergeant without pausing for breath. Despite their obvious distress, they were accused of having an overactive imagination but the police did reluctantly agree to accompany them back to the hotel to check out their story.

When they all returned to the room, they found the floor to be perfectly normal and solid enough. The couple could see that the police thought they were completely mad but they knew what they had seen and immediately left the hotel and stayed elsewhere.

Who's in the Family Grave?

In the 1920s, a man named Harold Smith died and his sons arranged for him to be buried in the family grave at Walton Cemetery but, when the grave was opened, they discovered an unidentified coffin lying on top of the two they knew to be already there. It was an expensive-looking, mahogany coffin with elaborate gilt handles, but it bore no nameplate. When it was opened, the Smiths were amazed to find a distinguished-looking gentleman of about 50, lying in its plush, satin-lined interior. On his hands he wore a fine collection of superb diamond rings. He also wore a costly blue velvet suit.

The appropriate authorities were contacted and they could not explain who the stranger was, or how he had come to be there and, as he could not be identified, he could not be exhumed from the family grave, which the brothers felt to be a totally unsatisfactory state of affairs.

On the following Sunday, the day before the funeral, they sneaked into the cemetery in the early hours of the morning and opened the grave once again in order to evict the unwanted stranger. As they carefully lifted the coffin out of the ground, they noticed that it felt considerably lighter than it had the day before – and when they prised open the lid, they soon found out the reason why. All that remained inside the coffin was the satin lining. The well-dressed corpse had completely disappeared. This mystery has never been solved.

Phantom Footsteps

In 1974, a street off Liverpool's Lodge Lane became the scene of a particularly callous murder. The victim was a beautiful young girl named Carol McLean, who worked in a nightclub in the city's south end.

The incident began one evening, when a man and woman called at Carol's flat near Lodge Lane, with robbery on their minds. Not long after Carol had opened the door to them, the couple started to ransack the place, expecting to find hundreds of pounds. They were to be disappointed as Carol only had a few coins in the flat. Maddened at their fruitless robbery attempt, the pair attacked her with a hammer, then stabbed her repeatedly with a kitchen knife.

Fortunately, the murderers were quickly caught and brought to justice and eventually given life sentences for their horrific and senseless crime. Meanwhile, back at the street where the crime had been committed, residents reported hearing strange noises during the night. The patter of light, tapping footsteps was frequently heard by the murdered girl's neighbours, on the landing just outside her flat. Carol had always worn high heels because of her job in the nightclub and the distinctive sound was exactly like the clatter of her stilettos on the tiles in the corridor.

Carol had often asked her neighbours to listen out for her when she came home from work because, on more than one occasion, men had tried to follow her back to her flat. The neighbours who heard the ghostly tapping of the high heels, noticed that the footsteps always stopped when they reached the front door of Carol's flat.

What Happened to Mother?

In 1889, a wealthy mother and her daughter from Heswall were returning from a holiday in India. They broke off the final leg of their journey in Paris, in order to visit the city's exhibition and they booked a room at a prestigious hotel. They signed their names in the register and were taken up to their room, number 342; a luxurious apartment, with heavy plum-coloured drapes, exquisitely-designed, velvet rose-coloured wallpaper and lavish furniture.

Within minutes of her arrival in the apartment, the mother fell ill and started to feel faint and dizzy. She was immediately put to bed and the hotel doctor was urgently summoned to her room. After examining her, the doctor called for the manager and, when he arrived, the doctor started arguing with him in French. The manager suddenly turned to the sick woman's daughter with a stark message.

"Your mother is seriously ill, Madamoiselle. The only medicine that can help her is at a doctor's surgery on the other side of Paris. I cannot leave her for a moment, so you must hurry at once to fetch the medicine."

The girl was in no position to argue, so she set out at once by carriage for the address but she had to wait for almost 40 minutes at the surgery, until the medicine was made up. Therefore, by the time she had returned to the hotel, almost two hours had passed. As she rushed into the hotel foyer, clutching the precious medicine in her hand, she spied the hotel manager and dashed up to him.

"How is mother?" she gasped earnestly.

The manager returned her entreaty with a blank stare.

"I have never set eyes on your mother, Madamoiselle."

"Of course you have," replied the exasperated girl. "We signed in this morning, right in front of you. Don't you remember?"

The manager raised an eyebrow but maintained his air of professional politeness and continued coolly, "You came here alone".

He then went over to reception desk and brought back the hotel register. He pointed to her signature and the girl could see that her mother's name was not there. The manager patiently watched as the confused English girl desperately flicked through the pages to search for her mother's signature but she could not find it. With rising panic, she took hold of the manager's arm and led him up to room 342 where she had left her sick mother. Upon opening the door of the room, the girl was startled to find that it bore no resemblance to the one she had seen earlier. Gone were the plum-coloured drapes and the rose-coloured wallpaper, gone, too, was the lavish furniture.

So the distraught girl suspected that the number on the door had been switched, but the manager allowed her to inspect every room on that floor of the hotel but none of them looked anything like the original room 342. The girl ran downstairs and demanded to see the hotel doctor. The man who had treated her mother just two hours earlier came to see her, but he also denied ever meeting either her or her mother.

When the girl returned to England, alone, she told the authorities that she believed that her mother had been kidnapped in Paris, but they did not believe her incredible story and, two years later, she was committed to a lunatic asylum.

There are a few theories that have been proposed as possible solutions to the mysterious disappearance. Perhaps the woman had contracted a highly contagious disease whilst in India, which could have resulted in the Parisian authorities being forced to close down the hotel if the story had come out. If this was the case, perhaps the hotel manager and the doctor had conspired to dispose of the woman – but how could they have redecorated and refurbished an entire apartment in a mere two hours?

The other, even more remote possibility, is that the mother was some kind of undercover spy, involved in a covert espionage mission at the Paris Exhibition and was subsequently 'eliminated' by enemy agents. This is pure conjecture and would still not explain how the hotel room could have been so radically transformed in such a short period of time. The whole case seems to defy all rational explanation.

Spirited Away

In 1878, Sarah Harvey, an 18-year-old Liverpool girl from Knight Street (off Rodney Street), went missing.

One evening she went up to her bedroom, full of pleasant expectation, to prepare herself for an evening out at the theatre with her young man. They were going to see a play at the Colosseum Theatre in Paradise Street and she was very excited by the prospect. When her young escort arrived to collect her, the girl's mother sat him down in the front parlour and trotted upstairs to fetch her daughter. She knocked on the bedroom door but there was no answer, so she opened the door and stepped inside. Sarah was nowhere to be found. There was nothing unusual about the room, a few clothes strewn about and various other articles such as combs, hairpins and ribbons just where her daughter had left them.

Then she noticed an upturned wine glass on the dresser and wondered who had put it there and why it was upside down. This part of the puzzle was solved the next day when Sarah's friend told her mother that they had been playing with a ouija board a few evenings before. There were no other clues to her disappearance and Sarah Harvey was never found.

Ten years later, a British team of explorers in equatorial Africa came across a remote tribe of pygmies. The tribe's witchdoctor, a very old man, was stretched out in one of the huts, dying. The explorers offered him some of their western medicine, but he refused. Shortly before he died, he made a startling confession through an interpreter. He claimed that, some years earlier, he had spirited away a golden-haired woman from a faraway island to his hut. Incredibly, he went on to say that her name was Sarah Harvey. One night she had escaped and run away from the witchdoctor whilst he slept and was last reported to be living with another African tribe in the Congo.

Can this strange tale possibly be true? Did the witchdoctor really teleport Miss Harvey from her cosy bedroom in Liverpool, to a mud hut in the dark continent?

The Human Hand

From the earliest times, the symbol of the human hand has featured in the culture and occult folklore of many nations. To primitive people, the hand was regarded as something magical, because of its ability to create tools, weapons and cave paintings and there is an ancient record of primitive man's reverence towards the hand in the form of a cave painting depicting an open hand on the wall of a cave at El Castillo in Spain.

In the Book of Daniel in the Bible, we have the first written record of a live, disembodied hand:

'In the same hour came forth fingers of a man's hand and wrote over against the candlestick upon the plaster of the wall of the king's palace. And the king (Belshazzar) saw the part of the hand that wrote.'

On another occasion, it is recorded that Daniel was touched by a hand that set him upon his knees.

In the Arthurian legends, there is an account of how Bedevere threw Excalibur into the lake and watched in awe as a hand emerged from the waters and grasped the sword.

The cult of the hand really took off in the 16th century, when the practice of robbing the right hand of a hanged man became a popular routine for superstitious criminals. After an execution, these ghoulish miscreants would wait for darkness, then raid the gibbet where a body was hanging. A ladder was placed against the gibbet and up would go a knife-wielding felon to hack off the hanged man's bound right fist.

The severed hand was later drained of blood and sealed at the wrist where a small wooden base was attached. Inserted between the second and third fingers of the dead man's hand was a candle made of human hair. Once lit, this unholy candle was supposed to ensure that all those who were asleep in a house being burgled would stay asleep. The logic behind this line of thinking seems ridiculous to the modern mind, but we must remember that, even today, there is a large proportion of the population which is gullible enough to believe in tabloid horoscopes – and this in the age of the computer!

Anyway, these hand charms were known as 'Hands of Glory' and the most famous incident of such a talisman being employed, occurred at Bowes Moor in North Yorkshire, around 1790 …

Hand of Glory

One night, a woman arrived at the Old Spital Inn (which lies about halfway between Barnard Castle and Brough) and requested a room for the night. After supper, the woman settled down by the blazing fire for a while and started to doze. The maidservant of the inn then noticed that the female traveller was wearing what looked like men's trousers and they were showing from the bottom of her skirt.

This naturally aroused her suspicions, so she also pretended to snooze in a chair by the fire, while she observed the mysterious traveller through partially-closed eyes. The man disguised as a woman, not realising that he was being observed, suddenly looked around, then produced a Hand of Glory. He lit the gruesome hand's hair candle and recited the spell that was said to unleash the talisman's power:

"Let those who rest more deeply sleep.
Let those awake, their vigils keep.
Oh, Hand of Glory shed thy light,
Guide us to our spoils tonight."

The robber then opened the door of the inn to admit several accomplices, who had been waiting in the shadows outside. Before they could enter, however, the vigilant maid sprang up, ran to the door and slammed it shut. She bolted it and ran upstairs to wake the landlord and his family, but she found, to her horror, that she could not wake them. As she shook them repeatedly, she could hear the gang of robbers outside, attempting to break down the door of the inn. Then she suddenly remembered that the only way to wake the sleepers from their unnatural sleep, was to extinguish the Hand of Glory's candle, which was said to be impossible unless 'blue' (skimmed) milk was thrown over the flame. The maid raced to the kitchen, sized a bowl of milk and hurled it at the grizzly hand and successfully doused the candle flame.

At that precise moment, the sleepers awoke and the landlord quickly picked up his gun and went to investigate the source of the commotion. Just then, the door of the inn succumbed to the battering and crashed inwards – but the landlord had reached the bottom of the stairs and blasted the intruders with his shotgun. They howled and fled into the night, peppered with shot!

Healing Hand

In the Lancashire town of Ashton-in-Makerfield, near Wigan, there is another dismembered hand, mounted in a glass case in the church of St Oswald. However, this hand was not used for stealing, but for healing. The hand is the relic of St Edmund Arrowsmith, who was put to death in 1628 for being a Catholic Priest.

Before St Edmund was hanged, his persecutors dragged him through the streets on a hurdle. Throughout his ordeal, the holy man clung onto two pieces of paper which contained the words of a prayer and an act of contrition. When his humiliating journey finally ended, he bravely mounted the ladder to the gibbet and was promptly hanged.

When Edmund was dead, the ghouls who were present cut him down, dismembered him, disembowelled and quartered him and tore out his heart. The priest's head was cut off and set on a pole amongst the pinnacles of a nearby castle. The judge who had sentenced him was very pleased with the way that the execution had gone and, with a sickening grin, picked up the dismembered parts of the priest and casually examined them.

Then, suddenly, he remembered something which the priest had said to him during the trial. On sentencing the holy man, the judge had said, "You shall die!" over and over, and the priest had responded with, "And you, too, my Lord, may die".

At the time, the judge had dismissed the priest's words as a treasonable remark, but, just over a year after the execution, he was sitting at supper, when he felt a hard blow on his head, as if someone had struck him with a fist. The judge swung around and, on only seeing his old servant at the other end of the room, he felt quite frightened. He asked the servant if he had seen anyone strike him, but he was equally baffled, as no one had entered, or left the room.

The next morning, the judge was found sweating in his bed with an expression of total fear etched on his face and he died shortly afterwards.

Relatives of the martyred priest managed to recover his right hand from the grisly remains at the castle and brought it, as a token, to his heartbroken mother. At around the same time, it was discovered that people suffering from a variety of illnesses, who touched the hand, became cured. The 'Holy Hand', as it came to be known, is still said to be affecting cures today. It is venerated in St Oswald's church every Sunday afternoon at 3.30pm, when the priest blesses those who congregate with the relic.

Strange Stories

Night of the Black Rats

Beneath Mason Street, in Liverpool's Edge Hill district, there is a maze of tunnels. They are the work of Joseph Williamson, or the 'Mole of Edge Hill' as he is known in local folk lore. Although he was born into a poverty-stricken Warrington family in 1796, Williamson rose from the gutter by sheer determination and hard work to make a large fortune for himself in the tobacco trade.

After coming to Liverpool, the 'Mole' devised Britain's first 'job creation scheme' in 1806, by employing the destitute souls trying to survive the slump in the economy which had been caused by the exhaustive costs of the Napoleonic Wars. Williamson assigned the men numerous pointless tasks and the most famous senseless work which he commissioned was the creation of a vast labyrinth of tunnels carved into the sandstone strata of Edge Hill. None of the navvies who burrowed their way for miles through subterranean Liverpool knew what the tunnels were for – all they knew was that Williamson paid them well to make them.

Today, the tunnels lie abandoned. Some are crumbling and others have been filled with rubble and refuse from various eras. This run down environment is a rat's paradise and in 1941, the detonation of a German landmine in Edge Hill caused a mass exodus of the rodent population. The landmine fell near Overbury Street, destroying St Anne's School. The blast burst the boilers in the school and a caretaker was scalded to death. The shock wave from the bomb simultaneously shook the sandstone bedrock of Edge Hill with a seismic jolt, causing thousands of rats to flee from their underground sojourn in fright.

Later that night, an old man was walking down Mason Street, when he saw what looked like a black oil slick, advancing down the cobbled road. He assumed that the black mass was some spillage from a tank that had perhaps been ripped apart by the bomb-blast. Then he noticed the thousands of pairs of red specks twinkling in the seething black tide and, with mounting horror, realised that thousands of rats were heading his way. They were large sewer rats which had been disturbed from their nests by the wartime bombardment. Although he was 73 years old, the man managed to shin a couple of feet up a lamp-post, just in the nick of time, as the sickening throng of squeaking, red-eyed rodents swept past beneath him.

When he looked to his right, he saw a vaguely amusing sight – a bunch of motley cats, perched precariously on a swaying tree branch, warily eyeing the plague of rodents. The felines, being vastly outnumbered by the rats, wisely stayed put up the tree!

Dead On Arrival

This weird incident allegedly happened at the new Royal Liverpool Hospital on Prescot Street in the early 1980s.

The double doors of the casualty department swung open one day and an unaccompanied man staggered inside with a badly bruised forehead and a bloodied nose. He managed to make it to the reception desk, where he informed the receptionist that he had just been involved in a car accident near Fraser Street and that he felt very strange. His actual words were, "I feel as if I am dead".

A nurse was called and she ushered him into a cubicle and sat him down and told him to take off his jacket, but he refused – he was too busy trying to take his own pulse. "I knew it! No pulse!" he declared, his eyes wide with fear.

The nurse eventually managed to calm him down sufficiently to take his pulse herself. She firmly grasped his left wrist and lifted the watch on her apron in order to count the beats – but there were none! This obviously shocked her but, before she could either make another attempt, or call for more assistance, her patient stood up and walked back outside. As he passed through the swing doors, he said to a passing ambulance man, "I feel as if I am dead and the whole world died with me". Then he staggered off across the car park before anyone could stop him.

Less than ten minutes later, the same ambulance man was called to the scene of a road traffic accident close to London Road. On arrival at the scene, he was confronted by the very same man whom he had seen earlier. This time he was lying dead in his vehicle. The postmortem established that he had suffered a massive heart-attack whilst at the wheel and had crashed into a concrete lamp-post. His forehead was badly bruised and his nose was bloodied and he was dressed exactly like the man who had visited casualty about ten or fifteen minutes before.

Modern-Looking Ghosts

When some people think of ghosts they tend to imagine them in the setting of the archetypal haunted house in the dead of night, with lightning streaking across a sky of inky-black cloud.

But there are many ghosts that choose to walk by day in such modern settings as car parks, offices, fast-food joints etc. Furthermore, not all ghosts walk around with their heads under one arm, wailing and clanking chains! Most ghosts can appear so mundane and solid-looking that they are often temporarily accepted as one of the living ...

In the mid 1970s, Nancy Dryhurst, a 20-year-old Liverpool woman, was about to start her first day of work in a warehouse off Stanley Street, when she was approached by a middle-aged woman in a red dress. The woman chatted to Nancy and told her that if she encountered any problems, she had only to come to her office for help, then she smiled and left.

Nancy presumed that the woman was either the boss or the manageress of the warehouse and later, during her tea-break, she asked a workmate what type of person the boss was. Her workmate described the boss as an old, grey-haired man who rarely visited the warehouse anymore. So Nancy asked about the middle-aged woman in the red dress whom she had met earlier. Nancy's workmate seemed puzzled and assured her that no woman of that age or description worked on the premises.

Later that day, another worker in the warehouse who was unaware of Nancy's encounter with the unidentified woman, jokingly told her about two girls, a couple of months back, who had left their jobs in the warehouse, after encountering the ghost of a woman in red. When Nancy heard this, she promptly took off her overalls and decided that her first day of work at that warehouse would also be her last.

Another modern ghost is reputed to haunt Church Street, one of the busiest shopping areas in Liverpool's city centre. Those who have seen this ghost, which is dressed in a pin-striped suit and wears glasses and a bowler hat, claim that the apparition turns into Church Street from Whitechapel between 8.30am and 9am on some weekday mornings and looks up at the window of a certain famous clothes shop with an expression of extreme terror on its face.

The identity of this spruced-up spook remains a mystery, but a man who hawks goods at a stall on Church Street informs me that he thinks the bowler-hatted figure is the ghost of one of the people who died in the fire that gutted Henderson's, an old store that once stood at the site of the haunting in 1960.

A New Awareness

In 1922, a dockworker from Stanhope Street named Peter Malone became depressed after hearing that his estranged wife, living in Wales, had been murdered. Someone had strangled the poor victim in her bed. Mr Malone had often visited his ex-wife, Liz, with his best friend, a clerk named William Jackson. It was the latter who saw his friend acting strangely one day, on the fourth storey of a waterfront warehouse on the corner of Wapping and Sefton Street. Malone had opened a small window and was sitting on the ledge, gazing listlessly at the cobbled street over 150 feet below.

"Peter! What the hell are you doing?" Jackson asked, putting down the ledger he was working on.

"Contemplating suicide my friend," Peter Malone said in a low despondent voice.

The gusts of wind from the Mersey ruffled his curled hair as he carelessly dangled his legs over the ledge.

"Don't be a fool! Think about your children!" Jackson tried to talk sense into his friend and started to cautiously creep towards the window.

"Stay there, Billy, or I'll take my life, I swear it." Peter Malone spat in agitation, as he leaned forward slightly and looked despondently at the ground far below.

"I won't let you take your life Peter!" Jackson persisted, poised to make a grab at the suicidal man.

Then, as Malone twisted to look at his friend, his left thigh slipped sideways and he felt himself begin to slide backwards off the ledge. His heart somersaulted and he heard his friend's voice utter "No!"

"Jesus!" Jackson exclaimed in fear. His friend was hanging onto the ledge by his fingers and his grip was slipping.

"Help, me" Malone shouted desperately, with a look of sheer terror in his wide eyes.

With a stony expression, William Jackson began to slowly smile. He avoided eye contact with his friend as he edged closer to him. He paused, then silently stepped over and started to carefully prise Malone's fingers from the ledge.

"No! Billy! What are you doing?" Malone, petrified, was puzzled and panic-stricken.

"I killed your wife Peter," Jackson announced with a trembling voice, still unable to look Malone in the eyes.

Malone could not comprehend the situation he was in, unable to speak he only returned a baffled expression. The harsh wind was pounding against his face as he tried to clutch onto the ledge.

Jackson kept on talking, his tone becoming more controlled and embittered. "I had an affair with her and she wanted me to leave Maureen, but I love my wife and kids." He stood up and stepped heavily on the remaining desperate fingers, "I had to do, it or she would have told Maureen." Jackson's voice quickened as he hastily explained, his eyes completely devoid of any compassion or emotion, as he kicked the last clutching finger off the side.

Peter Malone plummeted to the ground. As he fell, he saw Jackson's cruel face watching him from over the ledge as he descended to his gruesome fate. There was a dull, sickening thud as he hit the concrete, followed by an overwhelming deep sleep so intense that even dreams were absent. Neurologists refer to this curious state as 'awareness'. The most chilling form of awareness is when a patient under anaesthetic remains conscious but paralysed, able to feel every excruciating scalpel incision but unable to communicate to anyone. Malone was lucky to feel nothing. His only sensation was that he was drifting out of his body for a while, a peculiar rising sensation, which went on for an incalculable time.

The next thing he knew, he was regaining consciousness in a hospital bed. By some miracle, Malone had survived the fall, but it had left him without speech and his sight was lost in his left eye. Imagine then, how Malone felt when he awoke one morning to see that one of his bedside visitors was the despicable murderer, William Jackson, who had the audacity to bring him fruit.

All Malone could do was make incoherent grunting sounds. He tried to point an accusing finger at the killer, but could hardly lift his shattered arm. He was completely unable to reveal who his evil visitor was. Jackson seemed edgy as he whispered the same thing repeatedly in Malone's ear, "Peter, thank the Lord you survived. Do you remember me?"

Fearing for his life, Malone would only shake his head. Soon the day came when he suddenly regained the power of speech. It was during the dead of night. He cried out at the top of his voice and roused a nurse from her deserved slumbers. She frantically ran into the tiny room where Malone was being cared for, concerned by the persistent shouting coming from the bandaged patient.

Malone emphatically gave a full account of the confession his so-called friend had made and of how he had prised his fingers from the ledge instead of offering a helping hand. The police were soon banging on the door of William Jackson's home in Toxteth's Fisher Street. His wife answered and explained to the police that her husband had been missing for two days. A search was immediately launched for the dangerous Jackson, but he was never found. There were rumours that he had fled to Ireland. Others said that he had gone to London and was hiding out in Whitechapel, but no one was certain.

Peter Malone made a full recovery from his apalling injuries. The blindness afflicting his left eye was found to be only temporary and after a long period of recuperation he slowly began to lead a normal life again. In the latter years of Malone's life, when his children had left home and married, the old dockworker often expended his money in long drinking bouts in the taverns of the Dock Road. Despite his physical recovery, he never emotionally recovered from the terrible experience and when he died in 1946, he rambled on his deathbed about losing a wife and a friend, all in the name of love.

The Song that Killed

In December 1932, a down and out Hungarian named Reszo Seress was trying to make a living as a songwriter in Paris, but kept failing miserably. All of his compositions so far had failed to impress the music publishers of France, but he carried on chasing his dream nevertheless, determined to become an internationally famous songwriter. Seress and his girlfriend had constant rows over the insecurity of his ambitious life. She urged him to get a full-time job, but Seress was uncompromising. He adamantly told her that he was to be a songwriter or a hobo and that was that.

One afternoon, things finally came to a head. Seress and his fiancée had a fierce row over his utter failure as a composer and the couple parted with angry words. The next day, which happened to be a Sunday, Seress sat at the piano in his apartment, gazing morosely through the window at the Parisian skyline. Outside, storm-clouds gathered in the grey sky and soon the heavy rain began to pelt down.

"What a gloomy Sunday," Seress muttered to himself, as he played about on the piano's ivories. Quite suddenly, his hands began to uncontrollably play a strange melancholy melody that seemed to encapsulate the downhearted way he was feeling over his quarrel with his girl, as well as reflecting the dispiriting weather.

"Yes. Gloomy Sunday! That will be the title of my new song," Seress exclaimed excitedly and grabbing a pencil he wrote the notes down on an old postcard. Thirty minutes later he had completed the song, which was sent off to a publisher and accepted straight away. The music publisher told Seress that his song would soon be distributed to all the major cities of the world. The young Hungarian was ecstatic that he was finally achieving recognition.

However, a few months after *Gloomy Sunday* was printed, there were a spate of strange occurrences that were allegedly sparked off by the new song. In Berlin, a young man requested a band to play the specific tune. After the number was performed, the man went home and killed himself by shooting himself in the head with a revolver, after complaining to relatives that he felt severely depressed by the melody of a new song which he could not get out of his head. That song was, it was later discovered, *Gloomy Sunday*.

A week later in the same city, a young female shop assistant was found hanging from a rope in her flat. Police who investigated the suicide found a copy of the sheet-music to the jinxed song in the dead girl's bedroom.

Curiously, two days after that tragedy, a young secretary in New York gassed herself. Once again the mysterious song was referred to; in a suicide note she requested *Gloomy Sunday* to be played at her funeral. Only weeks later, another New Yorker jumped to his death from the window of his seventh-storey apartment after a neighbour had heard him playing the deadly song on his piano. Also, around the same time, a teenager in Rome who had heard the unlucky tune jumped off a bridge to his death.

The newspapers of the world were quick to report other deaths associated with Seress's song. It seems that the dangerous song affected listeners as far a field as Liverpool; in Toxteth one evening, a woman played a recording of *Gloomy Sunday* at full volume, infuriating and frightening her neighbours, who had read of the widely-reported fatalities supposedly caused by the tune. As the night went on, the stylus finally became trapped in a groove, causing the same piece of the song to repetitively play over and over. The neighbours were concerned and hammered on the woman's door but there was no answer. They forced the door open, only to find her dead, slumped in her chair from an overdose of barbiturates.

As the months went by, a steady stream of bizarre and disturbing deaths that were alleged to be connected to *Gloomy Sunday* persuaded the chiefs at the BBC to ban the seemingly accursed song from the airwaves. The deadly tune was not heard again.

The Afterlife Club

This is a strange but true tale of subtle deception which took place in Liverpool and Bournemouth in the late 1870s. In 1879, an army medical officer named Robert Jones died of natural causes. He was buried in St James Cemetery, leaving behind a 39-year-old wife named Violet. The marriage between Violet and Robert Jones had not exactly been a harmonious one. A tempestuous couple, they quarrelled frequently and Dr Robert Jones had been rumoured to be have been having an affair with an 18-year-old maid named Nancy.

A strange thing happened one Sunday, just a week after Robert Jones's funeral. Violet visited the cemetery with a wreath to place on her late husband's grave. She slowly gathered her thoughts as she approached the grave, still very upset by her sudden recent loss. Her attention soon became drawn to a sinister figure kneeling at the graveside in a long black coat. He was crouched up close to the stone, intensely reading the inscription on the gravestone. The stranger wore a floppy fedora hat and had the brim pulled down, hiding his eyes. Violet wondered if he was some relative of her late husband, but when she approached, the man in black turned towards her. On seeing her he bolted right out of the cemetery, almost knocking her to one side without even acknowledging her. The abrupt departure of the stranger made Violet feel uneasy and she drew her coat tightly around herself as she shuddered.

Months later, summer arrived and a shopkeeper named James Mooney started to pay attention to the widowed Mrs Jones. Within months they were courting, as Violet started to feel more like herself again after a depressing grieving period.

The couple booked into a very small hotel in Rhyl, far away from the gossiping tongues of Violet's neighbours. However, on the first night at the hotel, something extremely unusual happened. It was a very hot night, so Violet asked James to open the window. He did so and the couple then cuddled comfortably back into bed. A gust of wind from the window suddenly happened to blow one of the curtains aside and they were startled to see a face revealed, peering in at them. Violet screamed hysterically; it was the face of her dead husband, the late Robert Jones. James Mooney also saw the face and he reluctantly went outside to see who the prowler was. When he checked, there was no trace of anyone there. Violet was sure she had seen the ghost of her husband and naturally felt very uneasy. She was unable to sleep that night, as she believed that he had returned from beyond the grave to haunt her.

Just over a year later, Violet married James Mooney and they went on their honeymoon to Bournemouth. Whilst walking along the pier at the seaside resort, Violet and James noticed a man with a bowler hat, who seemed to be following them.

James Mooney finally snapped and he apprehended the man. In the struggle, the man's hat fell off. It was Dr Robert Jones. A veteran of the Kaffir War, Jones knew how to take care of himself. He took a swipe at James Mooney and successfully floored him with a swift upper cut. As Violet witnessed the inconceivable episode she fainted, landing heavily on the jetty. As her new husband bent down to assist her, Jones sped away and vanished into the milling crowds. Mooney staggered to his feet and rubbed his chin. The force with which he had been hit had been very powerful, surely no ghost could throw a punch like that. He wondered what on earth was going on. Violet was bewildered by the event and dismissed her sightings of her late husband as a result of an accumulation of stress and guilt caused by her recent wedding. Distressed by it all, the couple avoided talking about the strange goings on.

It was five years later that the most peculiar incident occurred. Violet received a letter from her supposedly dead husband. It was a truly amazing letter, bearing a London postmark. In the letter, Dr Robert wrote that he was dying of cancer and went on to make a startling confession. He explained that he belonged to a group called the 'Afterlife Club'. He described how this was a group of people who had faked their deaths and then paid coroners and doctors to falsify burial certificates and produce bogus coroners' reports. He went on to explain how, sometimes, the bodies of vagrants were placed in the coffin of the person who wished to fake his own death. In some instances, stones and slates had even been placed in coffins. It seemed that the man in black, seen by Violet at her late husband's graveside, had been Dr Robert Jones himself, taking a vain look at the inscription on his own headstone.

In an attempt to justify his extreme actions, he confessed to Violet that he had faked his death in order to live with Nancy, the young maid, who in fact had later deserted him. Dr Jones had felt lonely and isolated and had therefore gravitated back to his wife Violet. He had become intensely jealous when he saw Violet with her new love interest and, unable to suppress his jealousy, he had started to stalk her.

There were many other supposedly dead people who returned to life. Some had faked their deaths to escape debt, while others wished to start again with a new wife, to escape the humdrum domestic routines of marriage. Many members left most of their savings to anonymous charities which were actually just a front for the Afterlife Club. The club had been founded in the Lyceum, but even today, little more is known about the specific goings on that surrounded it.

Furthermore, there is one strange epilogue to the above story. An associate of Robert Jones was one Thomas Williams, a businessman who ran several factories in Lancashire. Around 1885, Mr Williams amassed huge debts and became bankrupt. However, he resisted paying even a penny to his creditors. Instead he simply vanished. Most of his friends skilfully spread a rumour which claimed that Williams had committed suicide as a result of his financial troubles. Yet, interestingly, the body of Thomas Williams was never found.

However, in July 1945, the skeleton of a Victorian man in tattered clothing was found inside a metal cylinder by a group of children playing in Liverpool. The cylinder was on blitzed wasteland, near Great Homer Street. A pathologist who examined the sparse remains found several documents in the clothes of the canned cadaver. They referred to a Mr TC Williams of Leeds Street (see the full account in Haunted Liverpool 1). Diaries covering the period of June 1884 to July 1885 were also found on the brittle skeleton.

No one has ever been able to explain why Mr Williams was in a cylinder, or how he died, but could he be the same Thomas Williams who vanished in 1885? We may learn more about the Afterlife Club one day.

The Phantom Trousers

Since January 1977, a surreal, supernatural apparition has been terrifying night staff at the National Giro Centre in Bridle Road, Bootle – in the form of a spectral pair of pinstriped trousers.

Security guards were the first to encounter the ghostly outline of the trousered legs, walking around the fourth floor of the building at around 3am. Early morning cleaners have also spotted the strange entity. Rose Robinson and Vera Kirkpatrick were sitting drinking a cup of coffee on the fourth floor, when they were suddenly confronted by a pair of pinstriped trousers standing in front of them in the corridor. They could also see that the partially visible ghost was wearing shiny pointed shoes. Slowly, other parts of the ghost's body slowly began to materialise.

"I looked up and saw a woman's face," said Rose Robinson. "It was pure white and she was staring at something over to the right of me. Then I heard these footsteps going away down the corridor, but the doors at the end of the corridor didn't open."

Security guard, Vince Lever, came across the ghost at closer quarters one Saturday night when moonlight was streaming into the windows of the Giro Centre's operations block. By the light of the moon, Vince could see that the spectre had blonde hair and, on this occasion, she wore a red dress instead of the pinstriped trousers. He described the encounter to his colleague, Tommy McEvoy.

"The place was empty, of course, and I was walking up to the window. The woman was talking on the telephone. I quickly went to fetch another guard from one of the other buildings, but when we came back, she had vanished, and all the doors were still locked."

"It's always cold on the fourth floor, no matter what the weather's like," said Tommy McEvoy. "It must have something to do with the ghost."

When I gave an account of the Giro Centre ghost on BBC Radio Merseyside's *Billy Butler Show*, a listener who said his name was Albert telephoned me and explained that the spectre was the ghost of a woman who was murdered on the site of the Giro Centre in the 1960s. I have since contacted Merseyside Police and asked them to confirm Albert's claims, but they have not yet replied. If anybody does have any information about the murder Albert is referring to, I would be delighted to hear from them.

There are many other instances of partly-materialised ghosts in addition to the phantom trousers case. In the staff toilets of a certain supermarket in Liverpool, a pair of ghostly shoes have been seen walking about, detached from any visible body! It seems that some ghostly images tend to disintegrate after a length of time – a phenomenon which may be responsible for tales of headless phantoms and disembodied hands.

The Ghosts of Tedbury Close

On Friday 13 August 1971, the residents of a three-storey block of flats at Tedbury Close, Kirkby, asked a church minister to exorcise several ghostlike figures that had been seen passing through their homes regularly for over two years. However, the minister told the persecuted residents that he would not be coming to help them because he was convinced that the media would turn the exorcism into a sensational news item.

The minister's lame excuse was received with much disappointment and bitterness and so the denizens of the haunted flats arranged for a spiritualist to look into the matter instead. Meanwhile, phantoms continued to roam the landings, moaning and wailing and invading the flats every night. They would move furniture and objects around, open and close doors and cause havoc with anything electrical. On one occasion, two housewives were enjoying a chat and a cup of tea, when the record player suddenly switched itself on and began to blurt out loud music.

One of the most frightening episodes in the haunting of Tedbury Close took place one evening in the bedroom of the Melia family's young children. John Melia, a toddler of 22 months, noticed a misty figure near his bed and walked over to it, quite amused. Watched by his mother, the tot then attempted to talk to the elongated entity, which hovered in front of him and began to emit a faint, multi-coloured phosphorescent light. As Mrs Melia cried out in alarm, the iridescent apparition began to retreat and vanished through the bedroom wall.

On 19 August that year, Bob Cooper, a medium from the Waterloo Spiritualists Association, held a séance at the flats and claimed that a troubled spirit, called Daniel Mason, had contacted him. According to Cooper, the spirit of Mason, who had been an early 19th century farm labourer, was earthbound because he had been the victim of an horrific axe murder which had taken place on the site of the Kirkby flats one hundred years previously and he was unable to leave the place of his untimely death.

The medium also claimed that he had contacted another ghost which was haunting the close; the spirit of an 18th century minister, who was attempting to guide Daniel Mason from the earthly plane into the sphere we call the afterlife.

Bill Angus, another medium who investigated the case, said that he had made contact with the spirit guide and it had tantalisingly hinted of a terrible disaster that would take place in the flats in the future. The medium quizzed the spirit for more information on the prophesied tragedy, but he refused to say more.

The spooky turmoil gradually died down over the following months and the ghosts finally left the residents of the block of flats in peace.

Rocking Chair Ghost

Rather appropriately, the following ghostly incident took place on the evening of 31 October 1974 – Halloween, the traditional time when ghosts walk and witches hold sabbats.

Responding to the repeated requests of the people in the neighbourhood, two council workmen turned up at a derelict house on Edge Lane and began to board up the broken windows of the long-empty dwelling. Numerous children had been playing and making mischief in the house and a series of fires had reduced the building to a blackened shell. As one of the workman glanced through a hole in one of the grimy windows, he noticed a bespectacled old woman in a red cardigan, sitting in a rocking chair, knitting. The workman shouted to his mate, and then used his claw hammer to remove the board which he had nailed across the front door of the building.

To his surprise, when he stepped inside the house, there was no sign of an old woman, or of the rocking chair she had been sitting on. Perplexed at finding no one in the deserted house, the workman convinced himself that what he had seen had merely been a trick of the light and he and his friend quickly boarded the door up again. Nevertheless, just to reassure himself that there was no one there, he took one last peek through the broken window pane and was shocked to see the old woman sitting in the rocking chair once again, knitting away with a contented look on her face, as if she was in the comfort of her own home. He quickly called his mate to come and take a look but, as he did so, the ghostly old woman evaporated into thin air, along with the chair she had been sitting on.

Later that day, the workman was packing up and preparing to leave, when a woman from the neighbourhood approached him.

"About time you boarded that eyesore up," she said. "It's a health hazard."

"Too right, love," answered the workman. "Oh! By the way. Have you got any idea who used to live there?"

"Some old woman. Never really knew her though; she was a bit of a recluse. Some days she didn't even open her curtains. The local kids used to torment her something rotten. One day they threw a stone at her window and broke it, then ran and hid and expected her to come out and chase them, like she usually did."

"And did she?"

"No. After a while they sneaked back up to the window and peeped inside. There she was, slumped in her rocking chair, with her knitting needles and wool on her lap, not moving."

"Was she dead?" asked the workman, fascinated.

"Not half. It was horrible. One of the kids screamed when he noticed a rat nibbling at the old woman's foot. The police broke in and the place reeked – the coroner said she'd died from natural causes – been dead for about four days. Apparently the rats had come up from the coal cellar and nibbled at her toes."

"What did this woman look like when she was alive?"

"As I say, I didn't really know her. All I remember is that she always wore the same, hand-knitted red cardigan."

This reply shook the workman to the core, as he realised that he had seen what must have been the ghost of the old woman through the crack in the window. Within minutes, he and his mate were back in their van, speeding away from the boarded-up house on Edge Lane.

Ploughboy Prophet

The word prophet usually conjures up visions of bearded biblical characters from the Old Testament, but in more recent times there have been secular-minded individuals who have had the talent (some might say handicap) of seeing into the future.

One such seer was the Cheshire Prophet, an uneducated ploughboy of the 15th century, named Robert Nixon. Robert was born in 1467, the only son of a virtually destitute Cheshire farmer. Farmer Nixon had long since resigned himself to the fact that his mentally disabled son would never amount to anything in life, so he had put him to use in the field as a ploughboy. The unfortunate lad was frequently scoffed at by the locals and labelled 'the village idiot' because of the apparent slowness of his mind. His appearance also made him an object of ridicule as his head was unusually large and he had huge, protuberant eyes. Despite all the spiteful jibes he was subjected to, the ploughboy was good-natured and inoffensive and said very little to anyone beyond a simple "yes" or "no".

One day, out of the blue, Robert suddenly surprised everyone, by predicting that an ox belonging to a neighbouring farmer would die. Not long after he had uttered the prediction, he and a group of curious villagers watched as the healthy-looking ox in the next field collapsed. When the beast was examined, minutes later, it was found to have died from no apparent cause.

News of the uncanny prophesy reached the ears of Lord Cholmondeley, who sent for Robert and kept him at his estate for a short while. The country squire tried to encourage the boy to learn to read and write, but Robert resisted all attempts to be educated, so he eventually left the estate and ended up back at the handles of his father's plough.

A couple of days after leaving Lord Cholmondeley's estate, Robert was ploughing one of his father's fields, when he suddenly stopped mid-furrow and stared skywards with a gaping mouth. The farm overseer ordered him to get on with his work, but the ploughboy remained rooted to the spot, engrossed in something which he could obviously see in the clear blue sky. The overseer struck Robert with a strap and told him to stop daydreaming, but the boy was oblivious, even to the strap, and did not react.

For the space of an hour, the ploughboy stood gazing up at something in the heavens, which no one else could detect, until he finally broke out of his trance-like state and resumed his ploughing as if nothing had happened. The overseer was burning with curiosity and urged the lad to reveal what he had been staring at. Robert thought about it for a while and then replied enigmatically, "I have seen things that I cannot tell you and which man never saw before".

This esoteric answer shook the overseer, who was used to the boy's monosyllabic utterances. Not only that, the ploughboy's voice had assumed a new clarity and speed of delivery, so unlike his usual muffled speech. It was almost as if something, or someone, was using the boy as a mouthpiece.

There were further strange vocal deliveries from the farmer's son. One day, before a group of startled drinkers in the local tavern, Robert held forth for two hours, in the accentless voice of his mysterious alter ego, expounding about the 'history of the future'. This unbelievably comprehensive lecture included details about the rise of an individual named Oliver Cromwell, the Civil War, the subsequent beheading of Charles I, the Restoration of the Monarchy, the reign of William of Orange and the French Revolution. Towards the end of his epic discourse, Robert predicted the abdication of James II in 1688:

"When a raven shall build its nest in a stone lion's mouth on top of a church in Cheshire, a king of England shall be driven out of his kingdom to return nevermore. As token of the truth of this, a wall of Mr Cholmondeley's shall fall!"

Lord Cholmondeley heard of the prediction and laughed it to scorn. He examined the wall mentioned in the ploughboy's prediction and, finding it to be completely secure, he told his bailiff that young Robert would be wrong on this occasion. The bailiff laughed and nodded in agreement. However, the very next day the apparently structurally-sound wall inexplicably crumbled to the ground. The remainder of Robert's prediction came true centuries later, when a raven did indeed build its nest in the mouth of a stone lion gargoyle at the top of a Cheshire church in 1688 – a mere day before King James II was deposed. The dethroned monarch later died in exile at Saint Germain in France.

On 22 August 1485, the Cheshire Prophet (as Robert Nixon was now known) was ploughing a field, when once again he angered his overseer by stopping abruptly in his tracks. Before he could administer his usual swipe with the strap, Robert suddenly lifted his whip and started brandishing it about, as if it were a sword.

"There, Richard! There!" he shouted. "Now! Up, Henry! Up with all arms! Over the ditch, Henry! Over the ditch and the battle is won!"

A gaggle of farmworkers came running across the field and gathered around Robert, who was now standing inert, with a smile on his face. He suddenly raised his whip in the air and declared, "The battle is over! Henry has won!"

The farmworkers fell about laughing at the ploughboy's amateur dramatics. But these same peasants became curious two days later, when two travel-weary messengers rode into the county of Cheshire with important news – King Richard III had died at Bosworth while fighting the Earl of Richmond, now King Henry VII of England. When one of the villagers asked the messengers the exact date on which King Richard had died, he was told that he met his death on 22 August, the date the Cheshire Prophet gave his performance of the remote battle, by simultaneously enacting the event at Bosworth.

On the day that the messengers arrived with the news of King Henry's victory, the ploughboy became extremely anxious and he nervously asked several of the villagers if he could take refuge in their homes.

"Why? Who are you hiding from, Robert?" asked one bemused villager.

"The king's men!" he replied, "They're coming for me. They want to take me to the royal palace and if I go there, I'll die of thirst and starvation!"

The villagers could make no sense of the ploughboy's words. For what possible reason would the king want the village idiot? And, for that matter, how would a guest starve in a royal palace?"

A few days later, several of the king's men rode to the Nixon farmstead looking for the famous Cheshire Prophet. When they caught up with Robert, they escorted him to King Henry, who was fascinated by the tales he had heard of the idiot-genius who could foresee the future.

The king assigned a scribe to accompany the ploughboy at all times, to record any predictions he should enunciate. One of the first prophecies to be recorded by the scribe concerned a future event that apparently has not yet happened. Nixon prophesied that soldiers, with white dust on their helmets, would invade the country through a tunnel.

Before setting out on a fortnight-long hunting trip, the king left instructions with his cooks to give the Cheshire Prophet all the food he desired. The cooks initially obeyed the king's commands but, after a few days, they tired of the ploughboy's incessant greed and decided to lock him up in a heavy oaken chest, until he was really hungry, just to teach him a lesson. In the hustle and bustle of palace life, the cooks completely forgot about the tiresome ploughboy until, two weeks later, when the king returned and asked if the Cheshire Prophet had made any more predictions whilst he had been away. Only then did the cooks remember that they had locked him up. With great trepidation, they rushed to the thick-timbered chest and opened it to find that Robert Nixon had died from thirst and starvation. The Cheshire Prophet's prediction of his own tragic death had come to pass.

A Ghost Calls

Those with a true clear conscience never fear a knock on the door after midnight.
Irish Proverb

There stands a large house in Abercromby Square which was once visited by a supernatural character. In 1845, the owners of the house, a Mr and Mrs Bickerstaffe, made preparations to go on holiday to Scotland. Mr Bickerstaffe left strict instructions with his staff not to admit any strangers while he and his wife were away. Mary Hennessey, the youngest housemaid, nodded in unison with the rest of the staff, as Mr Bickerstaff rambled on, giving out his various directives. As soon as he and his wife were leaving the square in a hansom cab, Mary Hennessey poured herself a large glass of brandy and sat herself down in the kitchen with her aching feet resting on the warm hob, taking a well-deserved rest. The remainder of the staff decided to visit an inn, which stood in Mulberry Street, just around the corner, but Mary stayed behind to look after the house with the 70-year-old butler, Mr Rumboldt.

At 9pm, the front door bell jangled and Rumboldt went into the Bickerstaffes' bedroom and peeped out of the window. He looked down at the caller with an expression of terror on his usually sangfroid face.

"Oh no," he muttered to himself, "it's happening again!" and he rushed to the stairway and shouted to Mary. "Don't open the door!"

But Mary was already pulling the front door open. A tall woman, dressed in black, entered the house and brushed past her. Without a sound, the agile visitor seemed to glide up the stairs. As she neared the top of the first flight, she shouted, "The baby!"

Mary trotted eagerly after the woman in black. The uninvited guest went straight into an empty bedroom and let out a blood-curdling scream, which terrified young Mary. The sound of a window being hastily opened echoed through the empty room – then a sickening thud was heard on the pavement outside.

"Mr Rumboldt! What has she done?" Mary shouted up to the drawing room.

Rumboldt emerged, shaking slightly.

"Nothing," he said, "calm down."

Mary hurried down the stairs, yanked open the front door and ran down the steps outside, expecting to find the woman's body on the pavement but there was nothing there. Mary craned back her head and looked up to the drawing room window – it was still closed. The housemaid was obviously baffled, until old Mr Rumboldt came down to explain.

"That was the ghost of Mr Bickerstaffe's first wife, Eve," Rumboldt said in a morose tone. "She came in one day because she heard the sound of Henry – her baby – choking to death in the room upstairs. It used to be the nursery. By the time she had climbed the stairs, Henry had turned blue and was already dead. She was so distressed that she immediately jumped from the window and broke her neck in the fall. What you have just seen has happened several times before – a few months before you were employed here."

Mary immediately decided that she was leaving. The terrified girl had no intentions of staying in a haunted house. Mr Rumboldt persuaded her to stay, by reassuring her that the apparition only seemed to turn up on the odd occasions when the house was mostly deserted and, indeed, Mary saw the same apparition again, two years later, when she was the only person in the house. That was because the Bickerstaffes, the servants and the cook were attending the funeral of Mr Rumboldt.

It is said that Mary Hennessey was later dismissed from her job because she unwisely told Mr Bickerstaffe's second wife, Florence, about the ghost and Florence was not aware that her husband had been to the altar before.

Today, the house that was once the Bickerstaffes' home is the property of Liverpool University, and several members of staff and security guards in this building have occasionally heard the front door bell ringing when there is no one on the doorstep – no one that can be seen that is!

Killer in the Backseat

In 1962 Susan Manley, a young lady from Hoylake, met and married her husband, an American. Subsequently she moved from her home town to start her married life with him in Salt Lake City. One bleak night in 1965, Susan was driving home from her mother-in-law's house in a place called Ogden. About three minutes into the journey, she glanced in her rear view mirror and happened to notice that a white car was following her. A rational woman, she remained calm, but kept her eye on the vehicle. Turning off abruptly, she noticed that the car behind also turned. It then started to tailgate and whenever Susan speeded up, the mysterious car did the same.

Susan now began to panic. With horror stories of late night attacks haunting her mind, she leant over and locked the passenger door. In a desperate attempt to lose the predator, she took a winding route home, but this was to no avail as the car followed her down every lane and eventually onto the motorway. Suspicious and now afraid, Susan could not shake off the terrible feeling in the pit of her stomach. When she reached Salt Lake City, she started speeding through red lights to get away from the white car, but it relentlessly did the same.

Susan pulled hastily into her drive way. She felt petrified as the troublesome car also sped into her drive and pulled up along side her car. By this stage she was in a state of near hysteria, so she slammed her fist down on the car-horn. After some moments, on hearing the persistent noise, her husband ran out of the house and was alarmed to see her so upset. He angrily confronted the strange driver, "What the hell is going on here?" he demanded, as the driver scrambled to open his door in haste.

The driver's face was pale as he rushed from his car and tried to grab out at Susan, who was still sitting, shaking in her front seat, with the doors firmly locked. She tearfully shouted to her husband through the window, emotionally explaining that the man had followed her all the way from Ogden. Her husband grabbed the stranger forcefully. As he did so, the man whispered cautiously, "I followed your wife because I was going to work...", he gasped for breath as he was roughly shaken. He continued, "...as I got into my car, I saw a man sneak into your wife's car, just before she reached the car park. Check if you don't believe me"

Dubiously, Susan's husband loosened his grip on the stranger to yank open the back door of his wife's car. Much to the surprise of both Susan and her husband, there sat a young man with a shaven head. He was squatting behind the seat, clutching a knife as he giggled to himself.

It turned out that the odd young man in the back seat had been on the run from a local psychiatric hospital for over a week. During that time he had slashed a vagrant's face and had also viciously stabbed a dog to death. Susan, although shaken at the time, was grateful to the man who had followed her and indeed saved her from such a dangerous man.

This true story is no doubt the originator of many urban legends concerning the 'killer in the backseat'.

A Case of Conscience

One fine spring morning in 1849, a 29-year-old music teacher named Ann Hinrichson placed a notice in the front parlour window of her home at 20 Leveson Street, Toxteth. The notice advertised, 'Furnished Apartments to Let'. Her Danish mariner husband, John, was away at sea, therefore she was left for a good while with the task of running a household and rearing their two sons, five-year-old Henry George and three-year-old John Alfred. She was also heavily pregnant, expecting their third child. The only other person living at the house was the young and pretty maidservant, Mary Parr.

Within days, a 26-year-old Irishman named John Gleeson Wilson answered the advertisement. He called at the house to inspect the vacant rooms – the front parlour and back bedroom. Finding them to his liking, he paid a week's rent in advance and moved in immediately.

The following morning at 11.00 o'clock, Mrs Hinrichson went to the greengrocers in St James Street and ordered some potatoes. She then visited the chandlers to purchase two jugs, before heading home.

Later that afternoon the errand boy arrived at her house laden with the potatoes. Unusually, Wilson answered and received the delivery; his manner was abrupt as he hastily grabbed the delivery. Thirty minutes afterwards, the delivery boy from the chandlers turned up with the jugs. He rang the bell. This time there was no answer. Inquisitively, the boy peeped through the keyhole and saw what seemed to be two legs lying across the hall. With his curiosity triggered, he scaled the railings to look through the front parlour window. The scene in the house that faced the boy resembled an abattoir. In large, scarlet pools lay the bodies of Mary Parr and little Henry. The errand boy jumped down and, dizzy with shock, he ran to find a policeman. He found one in Great George Street and the two hurried back to the house of blood.

At around this time a little girl had arrived at the house for a music lesson. She also sensed something was wrong when she received no answer. A concerned neighbour smashed a window to gain access to the house. Within minutes, the policeman as well as crowds of people from the street, were swarming into the Hinrichsons' home. Mrs Hinrichson was found lying battered and stabbed in the hallway. In the parlour they found the maidservant, Mary Parr, suffering from horrific head injuries. She was at least still alive, but only just. Henry, the five-year-old tot lying beside her, was dead and coated in blood, a sight that forced a gasp from all who witnessed it. Down in the cellar, Ann Hinrichson's other son, John, also lay beaten and dead. His throat had been savagely cut from ear to ear.

The only clues regarding the tyrannous crime were a bowl of bloodstained water in John Gleeson Wilson's room, with a poker and tongs lying nearby, as well as the absence of a large sum of money belonging to Mr Hinrichson. The murderous lodger was nowhere to be seen.

Mary Parr was rushed to the Southern Hospital, where she slowly regained consciousness. Faintly, she murmured that Wilson had wiped out the family in cold blood. Mary then slipped into a coma and sadly later died. Within the hour, much police attention became focused on the horrific crime that was to shock Merseyside.

Wilson had sold several items from the robbery in a London Road pawnshop. Buying a disguise, he then fled to his former home in Tranmere, gloating as he escaped past the local police, who failed to recognise him as he boarded the Mersey ferry.

Wilson was smugly certain that he had escaped. However, on the first night he was back home, something very strange occurred. He sat greedily counting the money with the help of his estranged wife, who silently and fearfully suspected he was the fiend behind the massacre in Toxteth. All of a sudden, his face became ashen and he gasped out loud. Wilson saw the face of an old man looking through the window, which should have been impossible, as they were on the second floor. The ghostly man was pointing at him with an accusing finger. Wilson's ex-wife also saw the apparition and screamed out in terror. The phantom vanished, but was seen three more times that night. The third time, it materialised at midnight over the couple's bed, only this time it wore a judge's goat-hair wig.

Wilson fled from the house and at first light returned to Liverpool. He entered the pawnshop of a Mr H Samuel, in Great Howard Street, to sell a watch, but Mr Samuel's intuition told him the customer was the country's most wanted murderer and contacted the police. Wilson was taken into police custody, where he broke down and made a full confession. He was hanged in September of that year in front of 50,000 spectators. Interestingly, it is believed that his Tranmere house, where the ghost was seen, was once the home of an old judge…

Five O'Clock Shadow

Most people who enjoy ghost stories and folk tales are well-accustomed to so-called 'urban legends'. These are dubious stories that appear in a variety of versions. Examples of such tales are the totally unfounded claims that mice have been found in bottles of popular soft drinks, that Paul McCartney died in 1966 and was replaced by a look alike who is still acting the part and so on. Such modern legends may seem harmless enough, but some tales can be very libellous towards people and companies. For instance, in the late 1970s McDonald's had to officially denounce the widespread (and unfounded) rumour that the meat in its Big Mac hamburgers was being supplemented by worms! It was, of course, pointless for McDonald's to explain that, pound for pound, worms were actually more expensive than beef.

One popular urban legend, a story that is usually passed off as a real incident which happened to a 'friend of a friend', may have had its origins in the following true story, which happened in Liverpool in 1949. Being a main port, stories told by word of mouth in Liverpool soon travel the world. I think this story is the mother of many urban legends told the world over.

Appropriately enough, the date was 31 October 1949, the night of Halloween. A 40-year-old motorist named William Charnock, of Ennismore Road in Old Swan, decided he would visit his Aunt Verity in Knowsley. Charnock had to wear glasses when he drove, but couldn't find his spectacles anywhere, so foolishly set out without them. While he was travelling along Prescot Road on his way through Knotty Ash, he saw a woman in a long black dress standing at the side of the road, waving at him. He slowed the car and pulled up to see what she wanted. Winding down the window on the passenger door, the woman peeped in at him.

"Please may you take me to Manchester?" she asked, in a foreign accent.

Charnock explained that he was only going as far as Knowsley, but the woman did not seem to understand, she only leant her head to one side and looked at him quizzically. He opened the door and she climbed in.

"Oh. Thanking you, kind man," she responded, in a slightly gruff voice. She got into the vehicle clutching a handbag and slammed the car door rather hard.

During the journey, Charnock learned that the woman had come to Liverpool from Sweden by boat and had been trying to trace relatives in Knotty Ash. Apparently, she had been unable to find them and had been told by their former neighbours that the people she sought were now living in Manchester.

Charnock could not help making furtive glances at the woman. He could sense there was something strange about her. Her hands were rather large and the fingertips broad and square. Also, the straight brown shoulder-length hair looked to have a synthetic texture. Despite not having his glasses on, he also noticed that the woman had a five o'clock shadow of stubble, which was showing through the heavy make-up. In fact the stranger was obviously a man in drag and realising this, Charnock began to feel very uneasy. He wondered what was in the mysterious handbag; a knife? a gun? or was he just being paranoid? Was the passenger a mere inoffensive transvestite? He tried to be rational but could not lose the distinct sense of fear he felt.

Charnock quickly concocted a plan to get rid of the dubious passenger. Thoughts flashed through his mind: if he could maybe pretend his rear lights were on the blink, he could ask the stranger to go out and see if they were working. Perhaps this could then be his chance to drive off. Furthermore, if the stranger left the handbag in the car as he went out to check the lights, Charnock would even be able to drive off with the bag, to see if there was a weapon in it or not.

Now convinced this plan was his only escape, he slowed the car to a halt in a secluded lane in Knowsley, just ten minutes from his aunt's house. He feigned concern as he studied the dials on the fascia.

"What is the matter?" the odd passenger inquired.

"The rear lights circuit. I think they're off. Could you get out and have a look to see if they are working?" Charnock asked, his pulse racing with nerves.

The female impersonator returned a blank look, "What for?"

"Just to see if the lights are working," Charnock explained, suddenly realising that sweat was trickling from his forehead.

"You go," the stranger bluntly suggested.

"Yes, of course," muttered Charnock. He reluctantly had to go along with his own ruse, so he left the vehicle to make a false inspection of the rear lights. He considered just making a run for it, but the nearest police station was over a mile away and there was no one about to come to his aid. On top of all that, twilight was gathering fast. Charnock unwillingly returned to the car. After telling the eerie hitcher that the rear lights were working alright, he cautiously drove off.

Then events took an unexpected turn. A drunk stepped out into the path of the car, making Charnock swerve to avoid him. As a result, the car collided with the stump of an old tree. It was hurled into a 180-degree turn, until the vehicle slammed to a halt against the fence of an adjoining field. The androgynous man was thrown forward, causing him to hit his head on the dashboard. The impact dislodged his wig and the man shook his balding head, and looking side wards at Charnock with an expression of pure hatred, he reached for his handbag. Within a few moments bright car headlights neared the crashed car, making Charnock exclaim in relief, "The police!"

The costumed man squinted at the blazing headlamps approaching steadily down the road, then suddenly fled from the car. His long legs, clad in stockings, easily stepped over the fence and he vanished into the darkness.

William Charnock sighed with intense relief as the car came towards him. But it never stopped. The car passed by, oblivious to the crash and continued on down the road, deserting Charnock. The Old Swan motorist was shaken and he leaned forward to lock the passenger door before he too drove off, just in case the demented drag artist returned.

And he did return, seconds later. As Charnock tried desperately to start the car, the maniac in female attire screamed and produced a knife before stabbing at the windscreen and offside door. The insane man tried to open the door, pulling so hard on the handle that the vehicle rocked on its suspension. The engine suddenly revved to life and Charnock tore off down the road. He could not be certain, but the terrified driver thought he had pulled the transvestite along the road for several yards.

When William Charnock reached his aunt's home, he gave a rushed account of his ordeal and telephoned the police, who duly turned up and analysed the scrape marks on the bodywork of the car. The wig that had fallen from the creepy assailant was found in the car and was the only piece of real evidence that seemed to back

Charnock's incredible story. A detailed statement was taken from him, but the strange hitch-hiker was never found. Police began to wonder if the story had been a wild attempt at some Halloween hoax, but two other people later came forward to substantiate the account given by Charnock. Two dock workers claimed that a suspicious masculine-looking woman had passed them in a yard near the Trafalgar Dock. The description of the figure matched Charnock's description of the hitch-hiker, right down to the handbag. Much effort was made to find the violent attacker. Enquiries were even made at psychiatric hospitals in the north of England, but there were no reports of missing inmates.

The knife-wielding stranger had literally vanished from existence. However, he was allegedly encountered again on Prescot Road in 1951 and again in 1960, but police evidently never took the reports seriously, for on each occasion, the hitch-hiker had been reported on the last day of October, Halloween.

Katie

In February 1876, a 45-year-old Liverpool spinster named Elizabeth Corte passed away at her home in Aigburth Road. A paraplegic from birth, Miss Corte had been wheelchair-bound all of her life. She had been cared for by her younger brother, Frederick, along with numerous servants. At her sad end she had finally succumbed to leukemia. Elizabeth and Frederick were originally from Tranmere, but had moved to Aigburth after the death of their father in 1869. Sadly their mother had also died, tragically, in a house fire many years before and the two orphans had been exceptionally close.

Frederick, a 34-year-old bachelor, now felt lost without his sister. The only other company he had was the elderly maidservant Jane Siddon and the similarly aged butler Archibald Smith, known affectionately as 'Smithers'.

Life seemed unbearable without Elizabeth and Frederick began to take refuge from his sorrows in a daily bottle of gin. During his excessive drinking bouts, Frederick would wallow in self-pity and rant in a raised voice about the injustices of life. Why did Elizabeth have to die? Why was he alone? Jane and Smithers would retreat to the basement kitchen whenever the master of the house flew into such drunken rages. However, that spring something took place which was to change the grim outlook of the bereaved bachelor forever.

One gloomy morning, consumed with hatred and in a drunken haze, Frederick was throwing his deceased sister's wheelchair down the flights of stairs, barking at the maid to open the vestibule door. She obediently opened the front door, as Frederick got ready to hurl the wheelchair out into the busy street.

As he lifted the chair, he noticed a barefooted girl with the face of an angel standing in his way. She shivered on the doorstep, chilled by the March morning wind. Her scrawny arms were cradling a bunch of drooping daffodils.

"Out of the way!" Frederick snapped at her.

He raised the wheelchair six or seven inches off the ground and was posed to throw it.

The girl, who was aged about nine or ten, stepped aside and cast him a strange look. It was the enchanting yet condescending look on that young face which began to thaw Frederick's heart. He felt more like the child. Refraining himself from throwing the wheelchair down onto the pavement, he instead smiled and stooped over the diminutive flower seller.

"What do you want, little Miss?" he inquired.

"I'm selling flowers, sir," the beautiful girl told him. She then glanced at the wheelchair confusedly. "Please sir, if you don't want that, I know of an old man on crutches who'd be very grateful of it."

"Oh, is that so?" Frederick slurred.

The girl blinked a pair of large green eyes, shiny and watery with the biting wind , but she said nothing.

Holding the timid girl's stare, Frederick announced: "I'll buy all your flowers. Come in, come in."

He backed up into the hall, awkwardly pulling the wheelchair. Behind him stood Mrs Siddon, wearing a look of unbridled disapproval.

The little ragged street urchin remained rooted to the spot and was full of suspicion, "Come on!" Frederick's voice boomed down the hallway, as the maid reluctantly beckoned the child in with a single side ward tilt of the head.

The girl cautiously stepped into the hall. As she did so her hard-soled feet started to tread the luxurious carpet. Frederick treated the malnourished and anaemic daffodil-seller to a full English breakfast. She ate with her hands, despite the dissenting tutting of Mrs Siddons. Frederick found it all very amusing. He learnt that the young girl's name was Katie Corrigan. She claimed she was an orphan at first, but later slipped up and mentioned her father. She admitted that her father was a drunken bully who thrashed her and made her stand on the streets selling flowers she had picked from the park. Katie wearily showed them the calluses on her rough and dirty soles.

Frederick decided that the unfortunate girl was to be clothed like a princess. He made a long list of items that were to be bought: shoes, dresses, petticoats and even ribbons to lend a measure of neatness and respectability to Katie's wild honey-coloured hair. Mrs Siddon measured the girl's feet and the small circumference of her delicate waist. Smithers scribbled down the measurements and was afterwards given a small fortune to purchase the clothes and shoes.

Meanwhile, Katie was washed down in a bathing tub in the kitchen. When the girl was stripped, the maid recoiled in horror at the scars and weals that criss-crossed the poor child's back. Frederick was immediately informed. On hearing the terrible details, he quizzed Katie about her address, for he wished to inform the authorities of her barbaric father's whereabouts.

It seemed that Mr Corrigan resided in a dismal court off Mill Street in Toxteth. However, he was not there when Frederick Corte called to confront him. A helpful neighbour accompanied him to a nearby public house, where the brute spent most of his time. Frederick found him lying unconscious on the floor in the sawdust. Two inebriated women were giggling and trying to lift the child-beater.

Frederick knew it would be pointless trying to confront Corrigan in such an intoxicated state, so he returned home. On the way back, he thought about Corrigan's drunkenness and it made him fully realise how the horrors of drink had actually affected him. Later that day, the butler returned with the new clothes for Katie and the girl was transformed from a barefooted specimen of neglect, into a pretty and promising young lady. Katie seemed overwhelmed with excitement when she was brought before a full length mirror.

Kneeling beside her, Frederick tearfully clenched the thrilled girl's hand.

"Katie, if we asked you to stay with us, would you?" he asked in a broken voice.

Katie returned a puzzled look, as did the maid and the butler.

Frederick glanced at them, blinking to stem the tears welling up in his eyes.

"She could stay here, couldn't she? She doesn't have to return to ... to him."

"But, sir, we have no right to take her. We should inform the police about her father," argued Mrs Siddon, in a rational tone.

Smithers said nothing, but his sympathetic eyes spoke volumes as he surveyed Katie, who stood there, studying her shiny buckled shoes as if footwear was a novelty.

"Katie, please stay," Frederick pleaded again. This time a tear escaped and rolled down his face. "You can have anything your heart desires."

The girl agreed with repeated nods and the two embraced. This was the daughter he had longed for, for so many years.

Tutors were hired to teach the girl and she showed a remarkable talent for the piano. Within a fortnight she was playing Für Elise. She also performed elaborate dances which melted the hearts of her substitute family. The child settled in well, radiating contentment. Whenever Katie became excited, she would perform one of her comical dances or play Für Elise, much to the delight of her companions.

The child was an inquisitive youngster, eager to know all the details of Frederick's life. Why wasn't he married? Was he in love with a woman? Had he ever been in love? The harsh circumstances the girl had been raised in had robbed her of a normal childhood and left her with a mature head on young shoulders. Frederick himself seemed to forget how young Katie was and would often find himself confiding in her. He disclosed that he had feelings for a widowed woman named Gloria. The girl asked him if he had expressed his feeling towards the widow.

"That just isn't done Katie" Frederick had explained to her, sadly. "She lost her husband not more than six months ago."

His glance drifted out of the window.

Katie urged him to take flowers to Gloria, but Frederick's reply was as stubborn as before.

"That just isn't done."

'A faint heart never won a fair lady', Katie had wisely told him, which made him laugh. Where had the young girl heard that? The familiar adage made the bachelor ponder over the lonely course he was taking through life.

Meanwhile, Katie was soon reported missing by her father. The police surmised that the worst outcome had taken place. Weeks elapsed without a word and Frederick hastily made preparations to move to a residence in the north of the city.

However, things went terribly wrong from there. Katie became homesick and one afternoon sneaked out of the house. Her father was astounded when he saw the girl so dressed up and he angrily interrogated her about her three-week absence. Knowing that the kind gentleman of Aigburth Road would get into a lot of trouble if she gave any details about her unplanned sojourn, Katie claimed that she had been staying with a generous old lady in Birkenhead.

Corrigan, a sly man, took his daughter round to the pub, and taking full advantage of the circumstances, he pretended to cry with relief. This elicited people to buy him a drink for a while, but the act soon wore very thin. The clothes were soon pawned and it was not long before Katie returned to her pitiful state, collecting wood for her father to saw up and sell as firewood.

On Christmas Eve of that year, Frederick Corte saw Katie in Bold Street with her father and older sister. Mr Corrigan was drunkenly singing and Katie was gazing into a shop window, looking at the fine lace dresses that she had once worn, probably reflecting on the vastly different life she once briefly led.

"Katie," Frederick gasped, when he saw his lost 'daughter'.

The girl turned and her mouth fell open with surprise. She remembered him.

Oblivious to Corte's presence, Mr Corrigan turned and grabbed Katie by the wrist.

"Come here, you dawdler!" he slurred, as he dragged her off down Bold Street.

Frederick tried to utter the girl's name again, but was so choked up that the words died in his throat. He felt his heart burn with sadness as he watched the girl, who had been a shaft of sunlight in his grey world, walking away from him. Until the Corrigans vanished into the crowds of seasonal shoppers, Mr Corte could see the pale face of Katie periodically turning back to him.

Back at the house, which now seemed so empty and lifeless, Frederick despondently tore down the Christmas decorations and had the tree thrown out. The house became once again shadowed by his despairing mood. But the worst was still to come. Unable to forget Katie, a month later in January 1877, Frederick Corte donned an anonymous Ulster overcoat and put on a flat cap. He walked to the dingy court near Mill Street. Two men were transporting a small wooden box to a cart. The box looked like a child's coffin. Moments later, Mr Corrigan emerged from the court with just one daughter and she was not Katie.

"Who has died?" Corte asked a bystander, trying to pretend that the patent, terrible truth could be a misunderstanding.

"His daughter, Katie," came the reply.

"Cholera," announced an old woman standing behind him.

Frederick Corte felt numb. He did not even feel the tears pouring from his eyes as he watched the little wooden box being heartlessly shoved onto the back of a horse drawn cart. Affected by the terrible loss, he felt uncontrollably sad. For weeks, Frederick Corte once again drowned his sorrows in a bottle of gin.

Salvation came his way one spring day when he saw the daffodils in Sefton Park. He thought of little Katie, about her hardships, and his mind drifted onto the child's advice regarding Gloria. That little golden-hearted girl had wanted him to be happily married for some reason. Her wise words echoed through his mind. Feeling indebted to the girl, the saddened man felt that the least he could do was to attempt to make his and Katie's wishes come true.

So Frederick Corte paid a visit to Gloria one evening and laid open the contents of his heart. He expected rejection, but Gloria was flattered and, after a brief period of courtship, she became engaged to marry Frederick. The couple soon married and honeymooned in Paris. On the night of their return from France, something inexplicable occurred. Frederick kissed his wife good night in their bed and was about to fall into a much-needed slumber, when he heard a distant sound. Gloria sat up tiredly as she also heard the noise drifting into their room. It was the faint strains of a familiar piano piece which Frederick recognised as Beethoven's Fur Elise, the piece of music Katie would play when she was happy.

Medium Well Done

I have met quite a few psychics over the years who have been called upon to communicate with troubled spirits. James Byrne, a well-known medium, once met me and shook my hand. Seconds later, his face became pale and his eyes stared at me in horror from behind his thick-lensed spectacles. He suddenly said, "Please get in touch with me; I have to tell you about something". I sensed it was something negative just from his grim composure and sombre tone of voice. He hastily scribbled his home telephone number down and handed it to me. I never did telephone him, possibly out of the fear that he would warn me of something unsavoury looming on the horizon. In actual fact, later that year I lost my older sister. She died of a heart attack shortly before her fortieth birthday, despite the fact that she had had no history of heart trouble.

Another medium I have met on several occasions is Billy Roberts, a man who has been at the gates of death many times, due to a respiratory illness which has plagued him since his Wavertree childhood. I like Billy's honesty, which is a rare quality in popular mediums. I have taken Billy to places with a ghostly reputation and on many occasions he has simply and honestly stated, "I feel nothing at all".

Other mediums have improvised with colourful details when they have sensed nothing, but Billy simply admits it when he does not sense anything supernatural. On other occasions, he has been very tuned in to entities and spirits haunting a location, in fact on many occasions he has startled me by providing the surnames of deceased people connected to the site of a haunting.

Behind the working medium image, Billy Roberts is a quiet, well-spoken man and a serious student of the occult, who routinely talks about such esoteric concepts as the akashic records, chakras, psychometry and auras. Many mediums are in the game for the money, but I know that Billy has a genuine interest in the spirit world. He is the sort of person I could listen to all day, as he has a vast understanding of the paranormal.

I rarely use psychics or mediums during my investigations into hauntings and paranormal phenomena. This, frankly, is because I have never been impressed with people who profess to be in communication with the dead and yet always fail to produce specific details, such as a surname.

Many mediums I have encountered over the years have used little more than blatant hypnotic suggestion on gullible people who are genuinely seeking knowledge about loved ones who have passed 'over to the other side'.

However, in February 2000 I decided to give a psychic named Derek Acorah a try with a specific investigation. He was literally a random choice and when I asked if I could put him to the test by taking him to several well-researched haunted dwellings, with a view to contacting a supernatural entity, Derek was very enthusiastic about the proposal.

I knew he was a very busy man who had been consulted in Hollywood many times by show business celebrities such as Cher, Bette Midler, Demi Moore and many other megastars. I was therefore surprised to find that Derek was a typical down-to-earth Scouser, who had not forgotten his tough Scotland Road upbringing.

The rendezvous was 44 Penny Lane, the abode of a particularly durable poltergeist and also the premises of Property Line, a student accommodation agency. I had made prior arrangements with manager, Ronnie Kingsley, to open the shop on Sunday and as soon as Derek arrived on the premises, he zeroed straight in on the small back room, of what had been an epicentre of terrifying poltergeist activity since 1930. The room is now used as the shop staff-room.

What followed was both sensational and unexpected. Derek gave me the name of a man who had committed suicide at number 44, back in the 1940s. The living descendants of the unfortunate have asked me to refrain from giving his surname, so I have to comply with their wishes, but Derek not only revealed the man's name to me, but also told me the exact tragic circumstances of his suicide.

As Derek was standing in the room, a misty-looking form appeared in front of me and another witness. The presence almost solidified into what appeared to be a contorted, distressed face. Derek calmly informed me that this was a manifestation of the suicide victim. As everyone present became increasingly uneasy, the medium assured us that his spirit guide, Sam, was present and overseeing things. Seconds later, the eerie-looking face dissolved like a vapour and Derek seemed to be very pale and drained.

Once he had recovered back in the shop, he told me that there were more earthbound entities present, from different time periods. He also warned me that the embittered suicide entity would become hostile, because it had been disturbed and identified.

Less than ten minutes after Derek had left the room to visit another haunted site with me, there was a loud, nerve-shattering clatter in the staff-room. When the manager nervously went to investigate the empty room, he found a box of A4 paper had scattered its contents under a table. There was no apparent explanation for the random spillage. In response to this, Derek has organised an exorcism-style candle ritual to be held at the shop in the coming weeks, to move the disgruntled ghost and its ectoplasmic companions 'into the light.'

Derek's unearthly talents were later put to the test once more, in Rodney Street, where we scaled the twelve-foot wall of a cemetery to take a look at the pyramidal tomb of James MacKenzie, a Victorian whose spine-chilling shade has been seen by dozens of witnesses over the years.

The psychic impressions Derek received in the proximity of this tomb were not only uncannily accurate, they also seemed to answer many seemingly insoluble puzzles that had confounded me for years. These shocking and mysterious revelations may find their way into print one day.

Skyquakes
and Explosions

Phantom Cannon Shots

The one o'clock gun was a huge cannon situated at Morpeth Pier in Birkenhead. The barrel of the cannon faced the River Mersey and provided a time signal for the shipping trade for many years. Another time signal from Bidston Observatory used to electrically trigger the gun each day at precisely 1.00pm. Obviously it did not fire a real projectile, but a blank which consisted of several pounds of cordite.

This famous time signal was fired for the final time at one o'clock on the 20 July 1969. However, since the early 1970s, there have been numerous reports of a loud shot being heard in the vicinity of Morpeth Dock. For instance, in 1972, at precisely one o'clock in the afternoon, police investigated the source of a loud bang that seemed to come from Birkenhead's Bridge Street. The sound was heard and reported by many people in the area; some surmised that the old gun had been fired. However, the police checked and found that the gun had not been discharged. No explanation for the boom was confirmed.

In July 1974, again at one o'clock in the afternoon, scores of people in Birkenhead heard a tremendous explosive sound, which echoed across the River Mersey. The source of the sound was never determined, but was heard again on three more occasions.

Also, on the night of 6 August 1978, another mysterious explosion, of a much greater magnitude, was heard over Merseyside and the surrounding counties, within a ten mile radius in fact. *The Liverpool Echo* reported the incident and told how the ground shook all over the region when the mystery explosion was heard. People came forward to describe the effects of the mysterious blast, which included the wardrobe mirror of a house in Liverpool's Lee Park being split in two by the tremor, as well as veranda doors at a house in Crosby being thrown open with the blast.

To explain the immense sound, a sonic boom from Concorde was blamed, but in actual fact the supersonic airliners were all on the ground at the time. Oil companies drilling in Liverpool Bay were also investigated, but after investigation it was found that they were not to blame either. Whatever rocked Merseyside that day was never identified. Strangely enough, a second so-called 'sky quake' was heard during the daytime later that year.

Strange Sounds

Another mysterious sky-boom was also heard over the north west on 23 January 1974. The epicentre of the blast was a small area of the Berwyn Mountains near Llandrillo in Clwyd, Wales. The blast was heard at precisely 8.38pm and was even registered by the Global Seismology Unit of the Institute of Geological Science, in Edinburgh. Strange lights in the sky over Merseyside, Cheshire and Wales were seen shortly before the titanic explosion, causing controversial tales to circulate afterwards of a UFO 'the size of the Albert Hall' which had apparently crashed into a hillside in the Berwyn Mountains. A nurse in the area claimed that she had seen the bodies of aliens scattered about the crash site. There were also reports from many other people in North Wales who came forward and claimed to have seen an incandescent flying saucer fall from the night sky. That night, the army arrived at the scene of the blast and cordoned off the area. Nothing more is known...

Near Death Experiences

Back From the Other Side

Perhaps this world is another planet's hell
Aldous Huxley

Like many people in the northwest, I always tune in to listen to the psychic, James Byrne, (who is regularly featured on Radio Merseyside). I have, like most people, often wondered what it is like on the 'other side'. Here are several near-death experiences (NDEs) which I have researched, in which people give tantalising accounts of what they saw on the other side. Most are pleasant descriptions of the hereafter, but the last one could be straight out of a Clive Barker novel.

In the autumn of 1968, a Liverpool-born army doctor was posted to a small unit in the foothills of the Himalayas. One of his first cases was a little girl of three, who appeared to have advanced meningitis. The young girl had slipped into unconsciousness, so the doctor administered a respiratory stimulant to her mouth, but that failed to work and her heart stopped.

The mother cried out, "Please come back," and, as she sobbed, she called her deceased daughter's name over and over again, tightly clutching the child's body. About ten minutes later, the doctor sympathetically guided her away from the child. However, the distressed mother struggled and ran back to the child's bedside. In desperation she grabbed the bottle containing the breathing stimulant and poured the fluid into her daughter's pale mouth. The doctor was very angered by this and tried to force the poor confused woman away. Amidst the emotional struggle, the little girl's eyelids began to flicker and she drowsily woke up, after her heart had been stopped for a full 15 minutes, amazing all who were in the room with her.

The girl explained that she had been to a place called 'Haven' and had had to pass through space and lots of stars to get there. She described how on Haven, there were strange flowers and trees that glowed beautifully. Even the grass gave off a greenish light. The girl added that she had met people who had been dead for thousands of years; she spoke of a man named Plato and someone else who she said had told her he had been a famous painter. She described to her mother how, while she was there, an old man with a droopy moustache had come up to her and embraced her, saying he was her grandfather. The girl also claimed to have met God, whom she described as, "funny, like a bit of blue sky with no face".

The girl went on to explain how she had heard her mother calling her tearfully. Apparently, at that very moment, within the haze of her unbelievable experience, she seemed to suddenly shoot off backwards, towards her mother's voice.

After the near-death encounter, the girl found that she suddenly had the ability to draw and crayon complex pictures of the place she called Haven and also the people she had met there. From her pictorial descriptions, these people looked like a group of ancient Greek philosophers. When she later sketched the man with the droopy moustache, he certainly did resemble her grandfather, who had passed away months before his granddaughter had been born. When her grandmother brought a photograph to compare it to the sketch, the two were almost identical.

The girl's story was featured on a British television documentary and the BBC's telephone switchboard was flooded with calls from people who had also had similar near-death experiences and these people claimed that they recognised the little girl's pictures of Haven. All accounts of the place sounded similar, a little like a traditional Christian Utopian version of Heaven.

Deathly Protection

Strangely, similar to the young girl's experience, in the early 1970s, a 12-year-old boy named David, from Colwyn Bay, was knocked down by a car. He was rushed to hospital, where the doctors fought what seemed like a losing battle to keep him alive. Their attempts to sustain his life failed and he died, without regaining consciousness. His brain was dead according to the EEG machine and his heart had stopped, leaving no signs of life whatsoever in the youthful body. The staff were dismayed by their failed attempts, as the corpse was tagged and wheeled out of the theatre. David's body was taken into a small room, while a nurse went to break the awful news to his grief-stricken parents.

Half an hour later, a doctor and nurse entered the room to take the body to the morgue. Much to their astonishment, they found him sitting up in bed. He was distraught and bewildered, tearfully calling out for his mother. Seconds later, a full medical team had been summoned to the room and, after a full examination, the child was declared to be completely fit and well. However, they were at a loss to explain how he had recovered.

That night, David told his parents how, after he had 'died', he had found himself inside a 'blackness' , which he compared to the darkness in his cellar. With a detached tone, the young lad explained how he had vividly seen a lot of faces of people who had died. These strange figures had started crowding round him, with laughing and jeering faces. He emotionally went on to explain how he had recognised one of them as his friend, Philip, who had died during an operation three years earlier. Apparently, Philip had defensively said to the other people, "Don't scare him, he's just come over. He's my friend". He had then turned to David and asked him to pray for him when he went back and then told him to comfort his mum and tell her that Auntie Sylvia was with him.

David then described how suddenly, a blinding light had shone down on the crowd and all the mocking figures had scattered. It was at that moment that David had woken up in the hospital room, all alone. When his mother heard the part about Philip's Auntie Sylvia, she convinced her husband to pay the dead boy's mother a visit, to tell her about the incident.

When the mother heard that her sister, Sylvia, was with her late son, the woman wept. She had told no one about the sister who had been taken into care when she was just five-years-old, although she had often wondered what had become of her. Now she knew. David's knowledge baffled her, but she at least felt comforted by the reassurance that her lost loved ones were united, wherever they were.

From that time onwards, David and his parents prayed for Philip's soul at weekly mass, just as he had requested.

A Great Shock!

In 1984, a Lancashire woman was trimming her lawn with a small electric mower. The blades of the machine accidentally cut through the mains cable and without a split second to react, the woman was electrocuted. The paramedics arrived within minutes, but, unable to save her after many attempts, the woman was certified dead and was taken to the local morgue.

Twenty minutes later, a renal specialist arrived at the morgue to extract the corpse's kidneys, as the woman had carried a donor card. Only seconds before the scalpel would have been inserted into the woman's back, she opened her eyes and let out a piercing scream. Petrified, she leapt off the slab and onto the floor where she immediately collapsed. One of the nurses in the room fled in terror, but the doctor acted quickly to save her life by massaging her heart and, after a short while, she regained consciousness.

The woman later told doctors that she had travelled down a tunnel of startling light (commonly reported in NDEs). After some confusing, but not frightening moments alone, she was greeted by a calming female figure who spoke to her gently. She introduced herself as Mary Lewis and then claimed to be her real mother. Before the woman realised it, she found herself in the morgue, much to her horror. It was later confirmed that, unknown to the woman until her strange experience, she had been adopted, after her natural mother, Mary Lewis, had given birth to her at the age of 17.

A Visitor from the Past

In the closing days of World War Two in May 1945, an 18-year-old Liverpudlian named Frank was fighting the Germans near the Black Forest. He was in a squad led by Sergeant Davies and, on one occasion, the squad was ambushed. A couple of Howitzer machine guns opened up and shot most of the soldiers from behind. Frank was hit three times and later likened the terrible, violent experience to being kicked by a horse. He hit the ground with a weighted thud and lay there helpless, watching his comrades dying all around him. As everything started to blur out of focus, he prepared himself for the fact that he was dying.

As Frank lay awkwardly in the foliage, he could vaguely make out the Germans running off into the distance. Then, suddenly, he perceived three distorted shapes right before him, that seemed to be hovering off the ground. The central shape, in soft focus, gradually became sharper. Frank could see it was a man of his own age, dressed in an old World War One uniform.

The ghostly youth approached him. He knelt by his side and calmly announced: "It's alright, Frank, you'll be OK. Just hold on".

"Who are you?" Frank asked, in much pain, feeling confused by the experience.

"Uncle Bill ..." he paused, smiling. "Help will be here soon, Frank," the figure stated reassuringly, before slowly vanishing back to merge with the other strange shapes.

Help did arrive. A group of men turned up about 15 minutes later and Frank was taken back to England, where a Harley Street doctor operated through the night to save his life. The very next day, his mother travelled from Liverpool to visit him. As she sat holding his hand, choked with emotion, Frank enquired about his Uncle Bill. She was surprised at the mention of the name and proceeded to sadly explain how Bill had been her older half brother. She then tearfully recounted how he had been killed in the Battle of the Somme. Frank was left bewildered.

Two months later, Frank's mother came across an old, dusty photograph of Bill whilst clearing out an old trunk. When she showed it to him, Frank was astonished to see that he was the very same person whom Frank had seen on that terrible night when he almost died…

Wanted – Dead or Alive?

In the early 1800s, a criminal named George Smith was wanted all over England for numerous crimes, including embezzlement, theft, forgery and fraud. Every time the authorities began to close in on Smith, he would fake his own death to escape! In fact, on one specific occasion in East Anglia, he actually arranged for an accomplice to bury him for an hour in a special coffin, with a tube affixed allowing him to breathe – successfully duping the law once again.

In February 1810, 'Lazarus' Smith, as he was commonly known, turned up at Liverpool, where he was planning to marry an elderly woman, after encouraging her to alter her will and allow him to inherit her savings. However, the heartless fiend was recognised by a man from Preston, who saw him one Sunday and gave chase. Swift on his feet, Smith speedily ran into St Nicholas's Church and mingled with the congregation to escape his pursuer. Only a couple of moments later, the spire of the church suddenly collapsed, killing 22 members of the congregation, including Lazarus Smith. As he exhaled his final breath, the last words he uttered were reported to have been, "I won't be returning this time". All the same, the authorities took the unusual step of burying Smith in a specially-reinforced coffin, just to be on the safe side.

Curiously, Smith was later reported by witnesses to have been seen holding up a stagecoach near Knutsford, in 1817. He was captured and after a series of police interviews he was later hanged. As he writhed in the gallows, he openly confessed to being Lazarus Smith, but nobody believed him. How could he have been Smith if he had been killed years earlier?

Loved Ones, Past and Present

The following account is a very old tale which I first heard when I was a child. In the 1880s there was a Doctor Charles Owen, from Rodney Street. Sadly, his wife, Sarah, died during the birth of their child. He was completely distraught without his love. One day the pain became too much for the heartbroken doctor. In desperation, he wrote a suicide note, telling his cousin to look after his child, Emily. An atheist, Dr Owen believed that death was final, full stop and it seemed the perfect end to his unbearable pain. Amidst his depressive state he prepared to drink prussic acid, but lost his nerve so instead injected himself with a full syringe of cocaine, a dangerously large quantity compared to the seven per cent solution used in surgery. He sat in his chair and braced himself for death as a terrible numbness filled his entire body. He fell into unconsciousness.

Next, Owen experienced the sensation of falling down a tunnel of light, where he then found himself standing in a field. In the distance he saw a breathtaking piece of architecture that seemed to be miles across. There was, standing gloriously before him, a series of high walls, domes and bridges made of a glittering type of golden-flecked marble. He could distortedly make out hundreds of figures walking near this colossal structure. Suddenly, someone called his name and, when he turned, there before him was his deceased wife, dressed in a silvery-blue, one-piece garment.

"Charles, you have to go home. Look after Emily," she pleaded. "Don't grieve for me. I'll wait for you," she said faintly, with a loving look on her delicate face.

Seconds later, the doctor was extremely bewildered as he found himself back in his surgery, where his brother-in-law and another local doctor were injecting him with drugs to counteract the overdose. Owen survived. As he focused on his surroundings he mumbled much of the vivid account to his companions.

Grateful for his chance to live on, as well as being much affected by his wife's guiding words, he proudly raised their child, although he still mourned his love and awaited the day when they would be reunited.

Years later, on his deathbed, just moments before he died, he smiled. As he did so he uttered the words "It's Sarah, she's calling me again." Once more, he gave a vivid description of the domed building, before he peacefully passed away.

Most near death encounters, especially those described here so far, are pleasurable. However, there are a few which have been extremely disturbing. This particular case was told to me five years ago.

From the Devil's Grasp

A woman from Old Swan was having dental treatment in the 1960s. She was unconscious because the dentist had anaesthetised her, using gas. Ten minutes into the treatment, the woman's heart slowed to a stop. The dentist frantically tried to resuscitate her, while the nurse rushed to phone for an ambulance. For three whole minutes, the woman's heart was not beating. By the time the ambulance had turned up, the dentist had managed to stimulate the woman's heart, which had miraculously started to beat again. As she came round, she had a very strange tale to tell.

She claimed that during the period of unconsciousness, when her heart had ceased to beat, she had escaped the clutches of the devil. Still frantic after her experience, she described how a large black hand had dragged her into what seemed to be a deep pit. As she had struggled, a man had stood by, laughing and saying the words, "We've got you now". She described this devil-figure as a tall man with a baby face, with intense, staring blue eyes. She insisted that he had no horns, nor a forked tail, but that he radiated what she could only describe as "an evilness" and she explained how she had just known instinctively who he was. The surroundings she had found herself in were very gloomy and she had heard disturbing wailing in the distance, so she presumed it was Hell.

The dentist dismissively told the woman that she had been hallucinating, but she firmly disagreed. Not a religious person, she felt so traumatised by the experience that she began to attend church. She put the unbelievable experience to the back of her mind and carried on with her life. One particular evening she was walking down Jubilee Drive in Edge Hill, on her way to mass when, all of a sudden a man emerged from a derelict house and blocked her path. To her horror, it was the very same evil presence whom she had encountered in her NDE.

Paralysed with fear, she let out a frantic scream and began to sob as the traumatic memories revisited her. The sinister figure paced up towards her, staring at her intensely. She panicked and slapped his face as he calmly stepped nearer towards her. The strange man reacted angrily and struck her, clawing her cheek, upon which, he ran back into the derelict house. An old man, walking his dog on the other side of the road, witnessed the harsh attack and ran to the distressed woman's aid.

Despite a thorough search carried out by the local police, there was no sign of the violent attacker in the derelict house. However, what was found there was a painting of a huge black hand on the wall of the parlour and below it were written the words, "Satan lives". Neighbours reported seeing a group of strange-looking people in the house a few days before, wailing and moving around with lighted candles. No inhabitants were ever located though.

After some time, a woman viewed the same house after it had been renovated. However, she later refused to move in after being disturbed by the 'ghost' of a man, whom she claimed to have seen in the parlour. She stated that his most disturbing feature had been his staring blue eyes, which had petrified her and troubled her for weeks afterwards. Could this be a coincidence? Or was Satan really conjured up?

Ouija Warnings

Bloody Mary

This is a grisly tale, told from two different sources; a man who worked at the Geemanco factory in Bartons Lane, Fazakerley in the 1960s – and a ouija board.

Before I begin, just let me issue a warning to the idly curious about misusing the ouija. Just as astronomy books warn amateur astronomers not to glance at the sun through their telescopes, I am warning novice dabblers to steer clear from meddling with the power of the ouija.

I have seen so any lives wrecked by the upturned glass and even one suicide, that I must dissuade people from playing about with forces they do not comprehend or respect.

Now that I have got that off my chest, let's get on with the story ...

In early 1996 I was observing a ouija session in south Liverpool. The glass kept spelling out a specific girl's name. The surname of this girl was very unusual and stuck in my mind. I scribbled the name down together with what her spirit had to say, with my usual unbiased attitude. The girl described how she was caught between this world and the next because she had died after being struck on the head in a factory in Fazakerley in the late 1930s.

I decided to research the story and, a week later, I was tracing people who had worked at this factory through a friend, who put me in touch with a man named John who had worked there in the 1960s. At that time it was called Geemanco and it was a printing works. John remembered that when he started at the factory, the guards seemed afraid to go near an old storeroom after dark, referring to an apparition they nicknamed Bloody Mary. John was curious about the nickname and asked why they called the ghost by that name. An old guard replied, "Oh, you'll see, lad, you'll see".

About a fortnight later, John was working on the night shift and could not help noticing that his workmates and manager were becoming increasingly uneasy as the night closed in. John needed to go into the old, poorly-lit storeroom at around 1pm to fetch a carton of paper – and there she was! A young woman, with a chalk-white face and blonde hair, standing there in clothes that belonged to the 1930s. Her blonde hair was soaked in blood and there were scarlet streaks down her face and neck. Her eyes rolled upwards and her mouth quivered. John still recalls the paralysis which gripped his legs.

"They just turned to jelly and I seemed to turn away from the ghost, which was about ten feet away, in slow motion. All I could say was 'No!'"

John finally regained control of his legs and described how he sped out of that storeroom at such a rate that he would have put Linford Christie to shame. The manager and his workmates calmed him down and reassured him that the storeroom was empty but he noticed that none of them would volunteer to go down to the room to switch the light off. For weeks after the encounter, John experienced terrible recurrent nightmares about the ghost, often waking in the night, in a cold sweat, screaming out loud.

When I told him about the girl's name coming through the ouija, John poured himself a large Scotch with a trembling hand and gulped it down in one go. He had given up cigarettes for six months, but was suddenly rifling through his wife's handbag for her packet of Embassy Regal. I went on to tell him that, back in the 1930s, a girl had been killed in that storeroom. She had been a factory worker, operating a large machine with an enormous eight-foot-long lever. This lever had developed a mechanical fault in its spring and one day it came crashing down, without warning, on the girl's head. One witness graphically described how the heavy lever had smashed in her skull, as if it were an eggshell. Amazingly, the girl did not drop dead on the spot but staggered around for a full ten minutes in a cataleptic state. Blood was gushing from the open wound in her head and her eyes were rolling about. The poor thing was unable to speak and presented a gruesome spectacle, terrifying her workmates.

A priest and a psychic were sent to the factory site recently and between them managed to induce her troubled spirit to move on from the place of her traumatic death, to what we would call the 'other side'. The terrifying ghost of Bloody Mary has not been seen since.

Troublesome Tampering

Whether you speak truth or tell lie is immaterial. Either will be contradicted.
Goethe

As Radio Merseyside's paranormal investigator, I get quite a mailbag and a plethora of phone calls about ghosts and supernatural matters in response to my regular slot on the *Billy Butler Show*. I have received an incredible number of calls and letters about dabbling with the ouija board. Without wishing to come across as a killjoy, I must warn amateurs that the ouija board is best left well alone, as it can literally result in the loss of life or sanity and I have experienced the dangers first hand.

I was once called to a house in Toxteth to investigate a poltergeist which had a habit of scrawling intimate details about an extra-marital affair which the female occupant, Mrs Smith, had had some years ago. Her husband and son had abandoned her as a result of the spooky goings-on and, in desperation, Mrs Smith called me at Radio Merseyside to look into the matter.

I must admit that, initially, I had suspected that she was simply an attention-seeker, until one evening, when all hell broke loose in the house before my own eyes. As I stood in the lounge, a pair of slippers quite literally jumped about on the floor. Stranger still, the mirror then flew off the wall and struck me with considerable force. Mrs Smith was on the other side of the room, screaming in sheer terror. Apart from the two of us, the house was deserted and empty. Then came the heavy thudding sounds of someone walking about upstairs. When I cautiously climbed up the stairs to investigate the source of the loud noises, there was nobody there. However, to my surprise, a mountain bike belonging to Mrs Smith's teenage son, Leon, was wheeling along on its own, as if someone invisible was riding on it.

Anyway, to cut a long story short, I discovered that the poltergeist activity had commenced shortly after Leon had started to dabble with the ouija board in his bedroom with a group of friends. Whilst tampering with the unknown, a man's name had come through, but the teenaged dabblers had become scared and turned the lights on after sensing an overwhelming, icy cold presence in the room.

Later that night when Leon had been sleeping in his bed, he felt a cold hand clutching at his throat. He immediately yelled out and the chilling hand released its grip. After much research, I have since found that, in the 1880s, a man strangled his wife to death in the same house. When I checked, the murderer's surname was the same as the one that had been spelt out by the glass on the ouija board. Since that time, Mrs Smith has left a bible on prominent display in the bedroom and, as yet, there has been no return of the poltergeist.

Deathly Drunken Dabbling

The dangers of the ouija board are further exemplified by this strange incident, which happened in Wavertree. In the summer of 1996, a group of men returned from the pub one night and decided to try the ouija for a laugh. Drunkenly, they cut out 26 little squares of paper and wrote the alphabet on them, in addition to ten pieces of paper containing the numbers from zero to nine. They dimmed down the lights and giddily asked if there were any spirits who had any horse racing tips. Within a couple of minutes, the glass inexplicably began sliding about, spelling out the words 'Fox Sparrow'. No one in the group had ever heard of a horse of that name and they dismissed the tip. Next the glass spelled out the words 'a dog three' which was equally mysterious. Unimpressed by the messages, the men drew the evening's activities to an end.

On the following day, the men kicked themselves when they learned that Fox Sparrow was the name of a greyhound which had come in first at a dog race. The number three had been the number of the winning dog. The very next night, keen to gain some racing tips, one of the men decided to test the situation. Again the men sat around the table, this time less jovial as they concentrated hard. As a tester, the intrigued man asked the board what his mother's first name had been. No one else present knew the answer, but the glass spelt out the name, 'Alice', which was correct. Naturally, the man was astonished by this and he decided to ask another question, so he jokingly asked how long he was going to live. The glass immediately spelled out the ominous message, 'not long', leaving a terrible silence among the stunned group.

Exactly one week later, the same man literally dropped down dead at his home, even though he was only 32 years old at the time. He had apparently died from a massive heart attack, which was a great shock to all who knew him as he had been a fit man, who had always played squash every week. None of his friends were tempted to try the ouija ever again.

The Devil Deceives

On another occasion, I received a call from a distraught young man who had been foolish enough to play with the upturned glass with a group of friends in Toxteth Park Cemetery, on Smithdown Road. The curious young man had asked after his grandmother, who had been dead for a year. The glass had slowly moved and then began to spell out accurate messages, which convinced the youth that he was communicating with the spirit of his deceased relative. As the evening wore on the messages became more complex. Then, late into the evening, he received a chilling message which convinced him that he was actually communicating with the devil, pretending to be his grandmother. The youngsters were terrified and fled the cemetery in such a panic that two of them narrowly missed being knocked down by a bus in Smithdown Road.

Let these cases be a warning to those of you who are tempted to dabble with the ouija board. It is not a game and meddling with the glass can end in death or derangement. A good friend of mine who has used the ouija for over a decade without coming to any harm, says he respects and understands the force that moves the glass. When the session is finished, he thanks the spirit for its service and bids it good night, then turns the glass over to 'release' it.

The practice of using an upturned glass to contact the spirit world is actually hundreds of years old. In fact, in ancient times, the shaven high priests of Egypt used upturned vessels to 'take messages' from the other world they believed in. The Druids also dabbled in a similar form of ouija and most occultists believe that long ago an ancient civilisation (now long extinct) which was more advanced than our own, perfected a way of talking to the dead through some hi-tech device and the ouija is but a symbolic relic of this long lost achievement.

Even today, there is an American electronics firm that has produced a machine called a 'Spiricom' which can allegedly send and receive messages connected to the spirit plane. I have heard tapes made with this device and you certainly can hear strange voices but they are very faint and there is also a lot of background hissing noise present. The device is an example of the controversial EVP (Electronic Voice Phenomena).

As early as 1920, Thomas Alva Edison (1847-1931), one of America's greatest practical inventors, announced in the staid *Scientific American* magazine, that he was working on a machine that would allow the dead to communicate with us. Edison's contemporaries thought that the 73-year-old inventor had lapsed into senility. Edison carried on working on his machine but unfortunately died before he could finish it.

However, it is the opinion of many modern researchers that Edison's views on the possibility of a spirit transceiver were vindicated in the summer of 1959, when a Swedish musician and film producer named Freidrich Jurgenson, inadvertently taped voices out of the ether, while attempting to record birdsong in a remote part of the countryside near his villa. On playback, Jurgenson was astounded to hear, not only the birds tweeting, but also faint human voices speaking in Norwegian or Swedish. The voices were not stray radio emissions, as the invisible speakers were discussing the birdsong.

The tapes attracted the attention of an eminent German psychologist, Professor Hans Bender, the director of a government-funded parapsychological research unit at the University of Freiburg. Bender set up a team of distinguished scientists to repeat Jurgenson's accidental experiment. The results were unbelievable. Disembodied voices were recorded and their origin could not be determined. Bender's team carried out further experiments.

They ran a factory cleaning-cassette through a brand-new tape recording machine in a silent studio. Upon playback, human voices, speaking unrecognisable words, could still be heard and Bender reluctantly admitted that the origin of these voices was inexplicable in the light of present-day science.

Many more EVP experiments have taken place since Bender's work in the early 1960s and experts say that anyone can record the strange voices, even on a common domestic tape-recorder. The best time to record them seems to be between the hours of sunrise and sunset. The tape should then be taken to a quiet room, or preferably somewhere in the country (to eliminate interference from man-made noises). It is recommended that the date and time should be spoken into the microphone before each session, followed by an invitation for the mysterious voices to speak.

Each recording period should be no longer than two minutes, as intense concentration is required in listening to the playback of the voices. Alternatively, if you have a radio/cassette recorder, you can have a go at taping EVP sounds by tuning your radio between frequencies (on FM if possible) where there is a dead band of white noise (which sounds like a hiss). If you then tape this noise, you may find that it contains voices upon playback.

Another similar technique involves wiring the ends of a diode (a cheap electronic component which is available from many electrical stores) to the wires of a jackplug, that is then inserted into the microphone socket of the tape recorder. According to EVP experts, diode recording gives the best results.

There is one curious aspect of EVP; the phantom speakers often talk at high speed, in sudden bursts and some psychical researchers believe this suggests that they lack the energy to talk at a normal rate. EVP research may one day lead to a technical breakthrough, which will allow us to communicate with the mysterious speakers. Whether they are the spirits of the dead, or beings in another dimension, is something else to be investigated. Strangely enough, the Vatican has shown a lot of 'off the record' interest in EVP and several distinguished and respected Catholic priests have even conducted experiments of their own into the phenomenon.

One of the earliest of these ecclesiastical experimenters was the late Professor Gebhard Frei, the cousin of the late Pope Paul VI, who happens to be the pontiff who decorated Freidrich Jurgenson (who practically discovered EVP) with the Commander's Cross of the Order of St Gregory the Great in 1969.

NASA has also shown a long-term interest in EVP. The results of the space administration's experiments have never been made public but, if a domestic tape recorder can pick up EVP voices, what can the sophisticated highly-sensitive recorders and equipment NASA has at its disposal detect in the quiet vacuum of space? Only time will tell.

Haunted Machines

A Ghostly Glitch

Most businesses today rely on computers in order to run efficiently and competitively. The ubiquitous silicon chip has almost put paid to the filing cabinet and the days of the Dickensian ledger book are numbered. This is the information age and if you want to get ahead in life, get a computer! Everybody is using them, even ghosts it seems, as in the following case.

One evening in May 1988, a cleaner in an architect's office in Stockport, Cheshire, was about to commence mopping the floor, when she noticed that the monitor of an unplugged Amstrad PC1512 computer was glowing. She was baffled by what she saw but, nevertheless, did not let it interfere with her work. That is until the next night, when the same computer, again disconnected at the mains, started to display unintelligible messages on its monitor screen.

The cleaner found it distinctly eerie, but later when she told other employees in the building what had happened, they just laughed at her. However, the following day a secretary who was using the possessed computer, nearly jumped out of her skin when the machine started to emit groans!

This prompted the office staff to seek professional help. Computer experts were called in, but they were unable to detect any trouble in the computer's circuitry. They checked its RAM and ROM, the microprocessor unit, disc drive and all the peripherals and eventually gave the machine a clean bill of health. But later, during the night, the computer once more reverted to its nerve-racking tricks.

Finally, computer pundit, Ken Hughes, the editor of *Personal Computer Magazine*, investigated the case of the rogue machine and set up a video camera to keep a constant eye on the monitor. Mr Hughes waited and waited and his patience was eventually rewarded. After nights of inactivity, the unplugged Amstrad computer suddenly crackled into life with what sounded like static electricity and its disc drive started to produce a whirring sound.

On another occasion, Mr Hughes watched in disbelief as the computer mysteriously turned itself on and began flashing random letters onto the monitor screen. He was the first to admit that he was baffled by these activities and that he would not have believed them if he had not seen them with his own eyes. He later took the machine to a computer exhibition in London, where the top computer experts in the country attempted to unravel the mystery once and for all. They stripped it bare and scrutinised every component of its hardware before reassembling it but, despite these drastic measures, even these technical whiz kids failed to explain the mystery.

A spokesman for Amstrad dismissed the unsolved case of the haunted computer as an 'amusing exercise' and the company reassured their consumers by issuing the brief statement that:

'If we seriously thought that the public were in any way worried that their computers could light up in the middle of the night, then, of course, we would investigate.'

They seemed uninterested in the potentially haunted computer.

The firm of architects later tried to sell the computer with a mind of its own, but could find no takers. The ultimate fate of the sinister PC1512 is unknown. Perhaps the entity which haunted the computer moved on to another machine!

Digital Dilemma

Stranger still, in November 1984, in Dodleston, Cheshire, there was a spate of poltergeist activity in a cottage being renovated by Ken Webster. Shortly after the outbreak, Mr Webster sat down at his computer to commence some last minute work. As he leant over to flick on his table lamp, he was astounded to see words being typed on the monitor screen. Confused, he stood back from the keyboard, staring in disbelief as the screen became filled with writing. The anonymous text read:

'Wot strange words thou speke, although I must confess that I hathe bene ill-schooled ... thou art a godly man who hath fanciful woman who dwel in myne home ... 'twas a greate cryme to hath bribed (Middle English for stolen) myne house.'

After recovering from the shock of watching the unusual message unfolding on the computer screen, as if it were being typed by invisible hands, Ken was curious to discover the identity of the phantom writer and nervously tapped this query out on the keyboard. The reply he received was completely unnerving. The entity communicating through his computer identified itself as Thomas Harden. After checking records, Ken was disturbed to discover that Thomas Harden was a gentleman of the 16th century, who had previously inhabited Ken Webster's cottage. Puzzling Mr Webster further, the spirit also chose to communicate by the decidedly low-tech method of chalking messages on the stone floor of the cottage.

The correspondence between the two men from different centuries is detailed in Ken Webster's book, The Vertical Plane. Many have declared the case to be a hoax and the alleged incident has been largely ignored by scientists. Despite scepticism, there is no explanation for these bizarre messages Mr Harden received.

House of Horrors

Another case of a possessed machine occurred at the Palace Hotel in Birkdale, Southport, in April 1969. It all began when a ten man team of demolition workers arrived at the thousand room hotel, which had been condemned. The workmen assessed their task and then began work on the gloomy old building.

Nine members of the demolition team had decided to sleep in the empty rooms of the hotel until the job was done, so later that night they settled down for their first night's stay. During the early hours, the workmen were awakened by a barrage of strange sounds which echoed through the deserted building. All of a sudden, the whirring of an engine sounded as the hotel lift began to operate – the doors slammed shut and it clunked noisily up to the second floor, which was where the eerie sounds seemed to be emanating from. This baffled the awakened men because there was not an amp of electricity in the place, as the supply has been cut off some weeks earlier prior to the demolition.

During the following nights, many of the workmen refused to stay at the hotel at night and went home instead. The brave few who did remain in the haunted hotel gradually discovered that, for some reason, the second floor of the building was the epicentre of all the supernatural phenomena.

Later, when the news of the haunting became public, a BBC television team turned up to make a documentary about the incident and the producer decided to bring a dog with him to see if the animal could sense anything. When the animal was taken to the second floor, it became very nervous and steadfastedly refused to walk down the landing.

The workmen decided to start the demolition work on the lift and began by cutting the cables. They were surprised then (to say the least!) when the four-ton lift refused to fall down the shaft. They made another attempt, this time cutting through the lift's main shafts. Still the lift refused to fall, seemingly suspended in mid-air. As a last resort, the gang of workmen struck the stubborn lift with 28lb sledgehammers for 25 minutes solidly until, suddenly, the lift plummeted down and hit the bottom of the shaft with an overwhelming crash. It landed with such force that it buried itself four feet into the hotel's cellar.

But that was not the end of the bizarre haunting. Exactly one year later, in April 1970, a fire of unknown origin erupted on the site of the old hotel and, on another occasion, some tremendous invisible force actually overturned a bulldozer right before the eyes of the startled workmen.

Some ghost-hunters have investigated this well-attested case. Their research suggested that the incidents were caused by the distressed spirit of a woman who, records revealed, had in fact committed suicide on the second floor of the hotel in the 1930s.

Unexplained Mysteries

Through a Glass Darkly

Mirrors are the windows of the devil
Leon Garfield

The following tale of prophecy has been circulating the south end of Liverpool for years. There are several different versions and, although each variation of the story gives different character names, the name of Mrs Prentice is always amongst them...

On the night of 14 April, 1912, the *Titanic* struck an iceberg in the North Atlantic, on her maiden voyage and sank, with the loss of 1,513 lives. When news of the unprecedented maritime tragedy reached Liverpool, everybody, especially the relatives of those who perished in the disaster, was saddened and very shocked. One person who was not shocked though, was Catherine Prentice, who lived in Upper Parliament Street, in the south end of the city.

Mrs Prentice, an elderly spinster, was regarded by her neighbours as something of an eccentric. She always dressed in out-of-date clothes from the late Victorian period and the curtains of her home were always tightly drawn. It was rumoured that she dabbled in the occult and some even suspected her of being a witch. One of her few friends was Mary Orme, an independent widow, who ran a local chandler's shop.

A few months before the *Titanic* made her doomed voyage, Mrs Orme told Mrs Prentice that her eldest daughter would be emigrating to the United States and would be making her passage on the luxurious White Star liner. When Mrs Prentice heard the name of the liner, her face became ashen and, in a broken voice, she warned Mrs Orme that her daughter, Grace, must cancel her voyage at once. Mrs Orme was naturally quite disturbed by her friend's entreaty and asked if she thought that something awful was going to happen to the liner.

Mrs Prentice foretold that the ship would sink after hitting an iceberg and that there would not be enough lifeboats to save all the passengers. Mrs Orme had long accepted that her friend had the gift of second sight and so took the chilling warning to heart. She pleaded with her daughter not to board the world's largest and most modern liner, but Grace was adamant that she would go and stubbornly refused to bend to her mother's request, saying that she was worrying unnecessarily. After all, it was a well-known fact that the *Titanic* had been described by her owners as unsinkable.

A fortnight before the doomed vessel was due to leave Southampton, Mrs Orme hid all Grace's savings from her as a last resort. This drastic measure had the required effect, but caused a bitter row to erupt between mother and daughter. However, when the appalling news of the great liner's sinking hit the headlines, Mrs Orme's daughter shuddered with relief and almost fainted from shock.

In 1917, Mrs Prentice suffered a major stroke, which virtually robbed her of her powers of speech. Her condition later worsened to such an extent that she became bedridden. As Mrs Prentice had no next of kin, she was tended by her only friend, Mrs Orme, and her daughter.

One night, Grace became tired of sitting at Mrs Prentice's bedside, as she seemed to be unconscious and she set off on a prying tour of the house. In an upstairs room she came across a crystal ball in the middle of a table which was covered in astrological charts of some kind. Fascinated, Grace tiptoed into the room and seated herself at the table and stared deep into the crystal ball. After a while, disappointed at seeing nothing, she grew bored and decided, instead, to have a browse through a bookcase of esoteric tomes of the occult, but soon found that they were too obstruse to be of any interest.

She was about to leave the room, when she noticed a reversed, oval-shaped picture hanging on one of the walls. Her curiosity was aroused and she turned the picture frame around. She soon discovered that it was not a picture at all, but a mirror. She gazed at her reflection for a moment, then saw a dark shape glide across the glass, making her visibly jump. Seconds later, the face of a man wearing a white tin hat appeared in the mirror. This apparition really frightened her and she stumbled backwards in alarm. The man's face in the mirror appeared to be talking but, although his mouth was moving, no sound was audible. Then the face vanished and a succession of other images appeared in the mirror. Suddenly, Grace saw something in the reflection which sent her fleeing from the house in a very distressed state.

When she arrived back home, crying and shaking, Mrs Orme immediately assumed that Mrs Prentice had died, until Grace told her about the ghostly faces she had seen in the bizarre mirror. Mrs Orme was stern-faced and angry at her daughter's prying behaviour and sharply told her that she should stop making such a fuss; she was simply overtired and imagining things.

Not long afterwards, Mrs Prentice passed away and, a couple of years after that, Mrs Orme and her daughter moved to Scotland Road, where they opened a small grocery shop. During the May Blitz of 1941, the two of them were sheltering in the cellar of the shop during an air-raid, when the building above them was demolished by a bomb, raining bricks and debris down on their heads.

After the 'All-clear' had sounded, Grace regained consciousness to find herself being pulled out of the rubble by a pair of strong hands. When she was back above ground and had wiped the thick dust from her eyes, she found that the hands belonged to an air-raid warden, who was smiling at her and asking if she was alright. She scrutinised his face which looked familiar to her. Then, to her horror, she realised that it was the same man in the white tin hat whom she had glimpsed in Mrs Prentices' mirror when she was a young woman. When she asked where her mother was, the warden slowly shook his head and told her that she had been crushed by a beam in the explosion and was dead.

Like many supernatural folklore tales I have heard, I took this yarn with a pinch of salt – until a couple of years ago, that is, when I read an intriguing manuscript in the main branch of the New York public library. The author was Bridget Hitler, the sister-in-law of the infamous German dictator.

In the manuscript, Bndget, an Irish woman who was married to Adolf Hitler's half brother, Alois, states that, in November 1912, 23-year-old Adolf, at that time a down-and-out, turned up unexpectedly at Lime Street Station, where Bridget and Alois were expecting to meet Anton Roubel, a relative of Alois. But Adolf arrived in his place, admitting that he had made the journey in order to avoid being drafted into the German army. Alois and Bridget gave him refuge in their home at 102 Upper Stanhope Street in Liverpool's south end. At this time, the area was a magnet for German immigrants seeking work.

Young Adolf spent most of his time in Liverpool wandering around the city, particularly the Pier Head and, as he was something of a painter, he often visited the Walker Art Gallery. However, as time went by and he contributed nothing to the household, he soon wore out his welcome as a lodger and Alois accused him of being a work-shy layabout. When he had first arrived, Bridget had tried to teach the young Adolf to speak English but she very quickly tired of his superior attitude, so he was left to his own devices once more. There was one person recorded in the manuscript who got on extremely well with Adolf – a Mrs Prentice – who was said to be a neighbour of Bridget's.

Mrs Prentice is described as an astrologer, who gave tarot card readings to anyone interested in having their fortune told. Adolf was apparently fascinated by Mrs Prentice's talents and, in the manuscript, Bridget Hitler writes that, in her opinion, Mrs Prentice converted Adolf into an ardent believer in astrology.

The Incorruptible

In January 1868, about 50 workmen were drafted in to dig up two thousand bodies from a part of St Peter's graveyard in Liverpool's Church Street. Some of the coffins dated as far back as 1707. All the bodies were removed with the utmost decency and propriety and were re-interred in Anfield Cemetery.

One particular coffin, which dated from the 1830s, was in an especially poor condition. It was so damaged that it split open as it was being transported onto a cart. To the absolute shock of the workmen, a fleshy body fell out of it. A murder enquiry was almost launched due to the state of the suspicious body, which fell out of the crumbling coffin showing no signs whatsoever of decomposition.

The fresh corpse was the body of a beautiful woman with long black hair, she seemed to have been aged about 25 at the time of her death. There was no rigor mortis evident in the corpse and a doctor was called upon to discover why such a fresh corpse was in a coffin which was almost 170 years old. The doctor reluctantly deduced that the woman's corpse was an example of a poorly-understood phenomenon called incorruptibility – a peculiar state in which the human body refuses to decompose after death. Many saints were incorruptibles, including St Bernadette of Lourdes, who looks as fresh and lifelike today as at the hour when she lay dying in 1879.

The mystery deepened when the name of the incorruptible woman was traced in the parish records. Her name had been Mary Edwards, a 27-year-old woman who had drowned in the Mersey around 1830. Research into rumours at the time regarding the girl's existence revealed a very interesting tale. Apparently she had been having an affair with a furniture maker named Mr Craven. The poor woman had been allegedly pushed into the river by him because she claimed to be carrying his child.

The mother of Mary Edwards, a woman of Romany descent named Edna, had had her suspicions regarding her daughter's death. After her funeral, she had gone into a public house where Craven was drinking. The enraged mother had walked up to the man and announced coldly, in full view of the pub, "My daughter Mary is lying in her grave, but she shall not lie fallow and perish. I curse the man who killed my Mary to rot away as he breathes."

Fascinatingly, over the next couple of months, Craven's health started to deteriorate. His eyes became sunken, his teeth literally fell out and he started to give off a terrible, sour-smelling odour, even though he washed everyday in a desperate attempt to rid himself of the awful stench. His hair had started to became detached from his scalp in large locks and he lost so much weight that he resembled a walking skeleton. Some said that just before he died, he confessed to killing Mary Edwards. Had Craven died of some poorly-understood wasting disease, or was Edna Edwards' sinister curse responsible?

The Amazing Mr Matthias

In 1972, it was reported that a very strange character visited the YMCA in Mount Pleasant. The unusual man had claimed he was a prophet and alleged that he had healing powers. He called himself Matthias and had long flowing black hair and an olive-coloured complexion. Numerous people in the YMCA confirmed that the man did, indeed, have amazing healing powers; apparently he also seemed to be able to read minds.

Stranger still, in one instance, a woman who cleaned the rooms at the YMCA said Mr Matthias had started bleeding at the wrists one Good Friday. Concerned, she had called for a doctor, before herself attempting to nurse the seemingly injured man. Both the doctor and also the manager of the YMCA, a man named Mr Pearson, allegedly visited Matthias' room and saw he was bleeding from his forehead and his wrists. Blood had also begun to seep through the man's white tennis shoes. The doctor examined the wounds and saw that blood was, unbelievably, coming from unbroken skin. In other words there were no physical wounds which could account for the extreme blood loss Matthias was experiencing. This phenomenon is known as stigmata. Throughout the ordeal, he himself had remained calm and silent, almost resigned to the gory experience

Matthias' bleeding stopped minutes later, leaving the doctor quite perplexed. Students training to be doctors at the YMCA at the time thought Matthias was just a conman or a sophisticated magician, because he had once performed a spoon-bending trick in the canteen. However, what they could not explain was how Matthias had actually done the Uri Geller-type trick without even touching the spoon. At the time, the gifted man had told one of the canteen staff to hold up the spoon, seconds later the girl had laughed out loud as the spoon had drooped right before her eyes.

Weeks later, the mysterious Mr Matthias suddenly left the YMCA unannounced. Staff at the hostel were unable to retrace him, despite persistent attempts. His present whereabouts remain a mystery to date...

The Ghost of Brougham Terrace

In February 1996, a security guard was dropping off a colleague at Brougham Terrace (the Registry Office of Births, Marriages and Deaths in the city). It was 6.30am on a freezing Sunday morning. As the security van entered the parking lot, the guards came upon a woman blocking their path. The driver was forced to a halt, and sounded his horn several times, but the woman just stood there, oblivious to their presence. She seemed to be aged around 45 to 50 years old and was wearing an outdated long blue frock, with a long silver fox stole draped around her neck. Stranger still, she carefully held a flower in one hand. The guard sounded the horn again and joked, "Come on, love, move! You can't get married 'til Monday!"

The woman finally began to move, slowly gliding towards the back of the vehicle, but when the guards jumped out of the vehicle to see what she was up to, she had completely vanished. The van driver realised that the vague lady he had just seen must have been a ghost and he felt very uncomfortable.

He revisited Brougham Terrace at the same time the following Sunday morning, armed with a camcorder, but the unreal lady did not reappear. When he enquired at the Registry Office about the ghost, he was greeted with a wall of hostile silence. He later learned, however, that the woman was the ghost of a cleaner named Alice, who had worked at the Registry Office until her death from cancer in 1983. She was always punctual and would be waiting on the steps of her workplace at precisely 6.30am sharp. The significance of her smart attire and the flower she was carrying remain unknown. However, her solid-looking ghost has allegedly been seen on six other occasions by staff over the years.

Phantom Airships

The silent heavens have goings-on.
Wordsworth

From 1909 to 1913, an armada of unidentified airships was seen in the skies above England. The first of these strange sightings occurred on 25 March 1909 in the town of Peterborough.

PC Kettle, a Cambridgeshire policeman, was patrolling Cromwell Road in the early hours of the morning, when he heard what he assumed to be the engine of an approaching motor car. As he continued on his beat, he noticed that the sound of the car had changed in pitch to a low buzzing noise, which now seemed to be coming from overhead. Looking skywards, Kettle was dazzled by a bright light shining down on him. The light was attached to some massive craft, which blocked out the stars.

The policeman could see that the silhouette was oblong-shaped, and he watched in total fascination as the craft suddenly accelerated across the starry sky in a southerly direction. Within a minute, the aerial light went out and the mystery airship was lost to sight. PC Kettle returned to his station and gave an account of the strange sighting to his superiors. He was not taken seriously and, instead, was ordered to take a couple of weeks' leave.

More nocturnal flights of strange aerofoils were reported across the land from Liverpool to Kent as the months went by and the newspapers were quick to nickname the epidemic of reports, 'airshipitis'. The aviation experts of the day initially dismissed the 'scareships' as collective hallucinations, despite the fact that these 'imaginary' invaders of English airspace were seen over towns situated hundreds of miles apart.

In the summer of 1909, the debunkers had a difficult job explaining away an unidentified airship which actually landed in London.

On the night of 13 May, a Mr Grahame and Mr Bond were strolling across Ham Common on the southwest outskirts of London when they noticed an unusual, cigar-shaped craft, approximately 250 feet in length, hovering about 12 feet above the ground. Grahame and Bond cautiously approached the awesome spectacle.

At close quarters, the two men could make out a couple of silhouetted people moving about in what looked like a gondola suspended beneath the underbelly of the craft. When they were 30 feet from the airship, the beam of a blinding searchlight shone from the gondola and swept the common, then singled out the two Londoners. Grahame and Bond stood rooted to the spot as two shadowy figures alighted from the flying machine and came over to meet them. One was a clean-shaven young man who greeted them with an American accent. The other occupant of the Zeppelin-like craft was a German, who asked for some tobacco. Mr Grahame produced a pouch of tobacco and handed it to the German, who held a calabash pipe in his hand. The German took some tobacco from the pouch, handed it back to Mr Grahame, then turned and headed back to the huge airship, followed closely by his American companion.

The American then climbed into a cage-like enclosure in the gondola and began to operate a series of levers that resembled draught beer pump handles. The German sat down behind his associate and began to study a large map dotted with coloured pins. The American pulled one of the levers down and the brilliant searchlight went out. The airship started to buzz, then gently rose into the night sky without either of the sinister aeronauts saying goodbye. The unidentified craft raced through the air in a north easterly direction across Richmond Park, towards central London, at an estimated unheard of speed of around 80 miles per hour.

Grahame and Bond informed the authorities, but their story was dismissed as nonsense and the staid editor of *The Times* refused to print an account of the Ham Common encounter, because he also thought that the story was preposterous. The French airships of the day were having difficulty achieving 30mph and the prototype German Zeppelins, hindered by poor aerodynamic design, could not surpass a 35mph limit. So who was the genius behind the unidentified airship that touched down in London?

Four years later, on the evening of 6 January 1913, a large, unidentified cigar-shaped airship was seen flying towards the coast of England near the port of Dover. Later that week, a dark cylindrical with lights on, was seen flying over the Bristol Channel. The same, mysterious, ghost-like airship was spotted a few nights later by a couple of Welsh policemen in the county of Glamorganshire.

But the airship gave its most peculiar performance in the skies over Liverpool on the Saturday night of 28 January 1913. Thousands of late-night revellers looked up to see the gigantic silent craft, silhouetted against the clear, starry sky. Many of the spectators began to panic at the sight of the stranger in the sky and wondered if it was some foreign airship on a mission to drop bombs on the city. No doubt there were some members of the public who had read *The World Set Free*, HG Wells' prophetic tale of a terrible aerial bombardment from just such a flying machine.

As the citizens looked on, a blinding beam of light shone down on the city from the airship, almost turning night into day. The beam swept across the length of the docks, then turned inland across the city centre as the awestruck public sighed in unison.

The immense spotlight settled on the railway network at Edge Hill, then flitted back and forth across Liverpool, focusing occasionally on various landmarks. The intense searchlight then blinked out and the sinister aircraft headed north and away from the airspace over the city, leaving behind a mystery that has never been solved.

Who were the sinister aeronauts who flew across the nation? The finger of suspicion pointed at Germany, but the zeppelins bore no resemblance to the giant airship which buzzed over the skies of England. One modern explanation is that they were UFOs, perhaps on some reconnaissance programme, who disguised their ships as dirigibles, so as not to alarm the local terrestrials, or interfere with their cultural beliefs. The extra-terrestrial hypothesis seems far-fetched, but it would at least make some sense of the airship phenomenon.

Mysterious Maid

The following strange tale was told to me by my grandmother, Rose Slemen, when I was just a child. I have heard many versions of it since and have also read an account of the story written by the distinguished crime historian, Richard Whittington Egan.

In March 1830, a young woman applied for the job of maidservant at a house in Islington Square, Liverpool. Her application was accepted, for although she was dressed rather shabbily, she had an honest and likeable face. Her name was Hannah Brade.

Hannah's employer – a widow who lived with her only daughter and young son – initially assumed that the girl was from the lower classes but, on many occasions during the maidservant's two years of service in the household, she was bewildered by her often unusual and uncharacteristically refined behaviour.

Whenever strangers visited the house, Hannah would become very nervous for some reason and seemed to be dreading the arrival of someone she did not wish to meet. As soon as the maid had reassured herself that the visitors were no threat to her and did not recognise her for who she really was, she would go about her business with regained confidence.

Sometimes the mask slipped. One day the widow and her children returned home from a day out much earlier than expected and were intrigued to hear the lilting notes of Beethoven's Moonlight Sonata emanating from the house. It turned out to be Hannah, sitting at the piano in the drawing room. When she suddenly noticed the widow and her children looking on in amazement, she stopped playing immediately and started dusting the ivory keys, flushed with embarrassment. When questioned about her obvious musical talent, Hannah skilfully managed to steer the conversation away from the subject.

The mysterious maid also refused to reveal how she had acquired her knowledge of medicine when she successfully treated the widow's son, when he went down with a serious fever. Within days he made a full recovery. The family doctor – who had warned the widow to expect the worst outcome for her sick son – was baffled by the boy's sudden return to health and was most curious to learn the ingredients of Hannah's top-secret remedy.

On another occasion, the widow's daughter found Hannah's exquisitely-executed pencil sketch of a rustic cottage, crumpled up in a bin. There seemed to be no end to the girl's talents and achievements. Another, even more startling accomplishment, was her command of several foreign languages. One day, at a market in the town, a German was asking for directions in broken English. Hannah, thinking her employer was out of earshot, began to converse fluently with the man in his native tongue. She was also heard singing away happily in French one morning, while she was cooking the breakfast.

Hannah soon became the talk of the town. Who was she? Who was she hiding from? She was obviously from a high-class background. How else could she have acquired such a comprehensive education? Was she perhaps hiding from justice because she had committed a crime? There were so many questions, but alas, no one ever managed to supply the answers.

One morning, the widow was saddened to discover that Hannah had packed up in the night and left the household. Everyone with whom the girl had come into contact missed her tremendously, especially the widow's children, who were literally heart-broken by the maid's departure.

Then, two months later, a mysterious package arrived at the widow's home, containing a number of expensive gifts. They were from Hannah.

From that day on, no one heard from Hannah Brade again and today, the questions remain unanswered; who was she? and why did she temporarily assume the guise of a maid-servant?

Was she merely a young woman from the upper echelons of society, sampling the life of the working class? To spend two years seeing how the other half lives would surely be a feat of stoical endurance for a young girl accustomed to the luxuries of the upper classes.

Sadly, we will probably never know why such a beautiful and educated young woman found it necessary to hide behind the apron of a maid-servant.

Into Thin Air

This story has been retold and mistold repeatedly over the years but this is the original, definitive version. Owen Parfitt was born in North Wales around 1700, but lived in Liverpool for most of his life. He had been a soldier, a sailor and latterly a pirate, wanted by the Liverpool authorities for inciting a mutiny and piracy. At the age of 55 he fled to Shepton Mallet, down in the south west, where he kept a low profile. As the years passed, his health deteriorated and he eventually became a bedridden cripple, nursed and looked after by his niece. He was unable to walk at all and became so weak that he had to be spoon-fed.

One day, he was sitting in his favourite chair, outside his cottage, passing his time by watching the passers-by and wagons trundling along the busy road. Eventually, his niece came out to check that he was alright and she saw, to her horror, that Owen Parfitt's chair was empty, the old man had vanished.

Three men who were thatching a house on the other side of the road told her how they had heard a strange whistling noise and suddenly, when they looked across to the cottage, Mr Parfltt was not in his chair anymore. No trace of him was ever seen again after that day. The superstitious believe that the Devil had come to take him, because of the crooked life he had led in his younger years.

Wedding Gowns from Nowhere

The following surreal tale unfolded in Birkenhead Park in 1991. That year, a member of the public drew park ranger, Dave Cavanagh's, attention to two wedding dresses, randomly strewn from a tree branch.

The ranger at first surmised that the dresses, which were of an old-fashioned design and made from ivory nylon with a lace top, had been dumped from a house burglary. However, when two more wedding dresses were found in the exact same circumstances in the following year, Mr Cavanagh realised that someone was playing an eerie game.

"They seem to be so carefully placed," mused the ranger, as he contemplated the odd situation, "someone is obviously leaving them here for a reason."

In August 1993, two more wedding gowns were found suspended from a branch on coat hangers, blowing about in the breeze. Again, no one was seen leaving the dresses there. In 1994, two more dresses, this time a bride's and a bridesmaid's, were discovered by 14-year-olds, Cheryl Jones and Mandy Morgan, who were walking near the park's old conservatory site.

This time, the bridal dress was made of the usual nylon with a delicately laced top and could have been bought in any bridal shop across the country. But the pink bridesmaid's dress, which had a sash around the middle, provided investigators with a clue to its origin, the label in the gown said it was made by Josh Charles. Unfortunately, lines of enquiry reached a dead end. As no one came forward to either claim or explain the dresses, it was decided that they should be given to a local theatre group.

And the Beat Goes On

This is a creepy story about something which happened around Halloween in 1999. Residents at a block of flats in Birkenhead complained to their housing association about the new noisy neighbour on the top floor, who kept playing Motown songs from 8pm into the early hours of the morning. Residents had tried banging on the door to complain, but the music seemed to die down whenever anyone approached the flat, as if teasing the complainant. None of the residents knew who the new addition was, but they had often heard him walking down the stairs at two o'clock in the morning, whistling loudly. Staff at the housing association dealing with the complaints were baffled, because, according to their books, the flat where the noisy resident lived was still unoccupied.

Assuming a squatter had moved into the empty premises, two officers from the housing association went to the flats to investigate. When they entered the flat in question, they found it was completely empty. It was in the unoccupied state it had been in since the occupant had died, two months back. Now for the weird part; when the two housing officers left the flat, and headed for the stairs, they heard loud music blaring out from the empty dwelling. It was that old song, *The Midnight Hour*, by Wilson Pickett. The officers bravely returned to the flat and as soon as they entered the hallway, the music mysteriously faded. Seconds later, the two officers heard footsteps pass by them and leave the flat. At first, the spooked officers wondered whether the inexplicable footsteps had just been in their imagination, until two residents claimed to have also heard phantom footsteps going down the flights of steps at that time.

It has since been established that, in 1996, a previous tenant of the haunted flat died actually on the premises, from a heart attack. Much to the annoyance of his neighbours, he had often played Motown songs on his CD player at full blast and older residents told how he also used to annoyingly whistle loudly as he walked down the stairs. So it seems that the cause of the footsteps could now be determined, but only through a supernatural explanation …

The Legend of the Old Woman in Newsham Park

A Lancashire folklorist recently telephoned me at BBC Radio Merseyside one afternoon and asked me if I knew anything about Old Mary, a strange old woman who is said to have been seen on the island in the middle of the boating lake in Newsham Park. I have heard about this strange character, but I assumed she was just one of those make-believe monsters of the mind, which children dream up to scare themselves. However, there were enough reports of Old Mary to send the police to the island on several occasions.

In 1959, two girls told of a chilling experience as they were playing on the island in Newsham Park Lake. As the girls giggled together playfully, they were startled to see an angry old woman, hunched over and draped in a black shawl. She signalled for them to leave the island. Amused by the agitated old lady, the girls just stared stubbornly back at her. However, the woman then started to chase them. Suddenly less amused by the scenario, they began to run away, now frightened by the mad lady. As they scuttled away, one of the girls screamed as she felt a hard yank on her hair; the insane woman had caught up with her and was grabbing out at her. Luckily, the girl broke free from the wretched grip, but in the panic of her scurrying away tearfully, she ran into the lake, desperate to get away. By chance, a man picnicking in the park saw the frightened girl floundering in the fairly deep water and dived in to rescue her as her friend cried on the lakeside. The odd female was nowhere to be seen.

I heard many more vivid reports from listeners when I mentioned the legend of Old Mary on the *Billy Butler Show*. One man in his forties claimed that he was getting goosebumps as he told me about the 'witch' who had chased him off the island in the late 1960s.

Just how someone could remain at large on a small island is a real puzzle, if we are to take the accounts seriously. Most of the reports span the years 1959 to 1968. Does anybody else out there know anything about Old Mary on the Island in Newsham Park's boating lake?

The Vanishing Prowler

Over the course of several months, from August to October 2000, I received a number of strange reports about a ghost that was actually encountered by the police.

At around 2.30am that August, an alarm went off in St John's Precinct. Security cameras showed nothing at first, then a couple of guards made out a solitary figure on a closed-circuit television monitor. The figure was of a man in curiously outdated clothes which looked as if they belonged to the 1970s. He had dark hair and wore a light brown jacket with flared beige-coloured trousers. The man was wandering aimlessly about at an upper level of the precinct at the rear of the Argos store. When the police investigated, the man had vanished.

Rumour has it that that specific section of St John's Precinct is haunted. According to many traders and security guards, strange noises on the upper levels have been heard, long after the place is closed.

The mysterious prowler, in out of vogue clothes, soon appeared again and once more set off alarms. This time, he was immediately apprehended by the police, as he stood outside the shopping complex. The suspicious officers quizzed the peculiar loiterer. He seemed to be sedated and spoke vaguely, as if he was under the influence of drugs. The police enquired who he was and where exactly he was going at 2.40am. The spaced out individual gave them the name, 'Richie', although another account says that the name given was Fitzy. It was also reported that the man had a card on him which read, 'Merseyside Artists Agency', or possibly 'Merseyside Talent Agency', with the name Don La Varo printed on the same card.

Richie, or possibly Fitzy – whatever his name was – then mentioned something which struck the officers as being utterly strange. He claimed that he had just come out of Bailey's nightclub. The police were puzzled, due to the fact that there is no such club in the vicinity. However, I have since learned that there was, in the past, a club of that name in St John's Precinct, near to where St George's Hotel once stood. Incidentally, I think that that hotel has now been demolished to make way for a car park.

According to two witnesses, as the suspicious man was being taken into custody for questioning, he vanished before the police officers' eyes. The police were naturally very shocked at the unexplainable vanishing act, and it was only then that they realised that Richie had been a ghost. For some reason, the ghost has been particularly active over the last three months, but the traders in the precinct claim that it dates back to the early 1980s. I wonder if any readers can throw any light on this ghost? Any information would be most gratefully received.

Merseyside Time Slips

"Scientific people," said the Time Traveller, "know very well that time is only a kind of space."
HG Wells, *The Time Machine*

Time is the perfect murderer. Every day it indiscriminately kills around 40,000 individuals worldwide. Rich and poor, black and white – all succumb to time's insidious erosion of their bodies and minds and it seems as if there is not a thing we can do to stop its merciless onslaught. People often talk of killing time, but ironically it is the other way round. If only it were possible to hinder the passage of time, then we could extend our transient lifespans. The Roman writer, Horace, succinctly summed up our mortal predicament in one sentence, over a thousand years ago: "Life's short span forbids us embarking on far-reaching hopes."

To stop the clock and live indefinitely has been a recurring dream throughout the history of mankind, but will the fantasy ever become a reality? It is the author's belief that the flow of time can be controlled and that, incredible as it seems, various individuals have inadvertently moved backwards and forwards through the 'fourth dimension' - the official scientific description of time. These time-walkers will be examined in this chapter, but first let us take a cursory look at the nature of time from a scientific viewpoint.

What we call time is still something of a mystery. Until the German mathematical physicist, Albert Einstein (1979-1955), came along, scientists regarded time as an absolute, universal, unchanging something, which flowed steadily on in one direction, like a mighty river, from the past to the future. Einstein proved that this was simply not the case at all. Long before experiments verified that his reasoning was correct, Einstein told the sceptical scientific community of his day that time was elastic, reversible and actually ran at different rates in different areas of the universe, which made a mockery of the traditional notions of time laid down by the English scientist and mathematician, Sir Isaac Newton (1642-1727).

Einstein's claim was regarded as being revolutionary, even nonsensical initially: objects which are moving, age more slowly than stationary objects. As an example, imagine a set of identical twins. One of them climbs aboard a rocket which takes off from Earth and begins a five-year space voyage at a speed very close to light's velocity (which is 186, 281 miles per second). By the time that the astronaut returns to Earth, he would find that his terrestrial twin is now 50 years older than him!

Einstein's incredible theory of time dilation has now been proved in many ways. If we had two, highly-accurate, atomic clocks and we placed one at an airport and one in Concorde and flew it to New York and back, we would find that the readouts from the two clocks would be different when they were subsequently compared, because the clock on Concorde would have ticked more slowly than the stationary clock in the airport. Time dilation has also been observed in sub-atomic particles such as the muon, which decays on average after 2.2 microseconds.

These particles are created when cosmic rays enter the upper atmosphere and are so short-lived that, in theory, they ought not to persist for long enough to reach the Earth's surface, but they do, because they are moving so fast that their time-scale, relative to ours, is slowed down.

If you are still not convinced that there is more to time than meets the eye, you should go out on a cloudless, moonless night and look up at the stars; you will be participating in a type of time-travel yourself, because you will be seeing the stars as they were many millions of years ago. If you see a faint frizzy patch of luminosity to the upper left of the Pegasus Constellation, you will be looking at the Andromeda Galaxy, which is the nearest galaxy to ours. But you will not be seeing this galaxy as it is, but as it was 2.2 million years ago, because it is so far away, that the light emitted from it takes that length of time to reach your eyes here on Earth. In other words, you will be looking back into the remote past when you look up into the sky.

Astronomers recently announced that a cluster of galaxies known as Abell 2065 had been discovered in the Corona Borealis Constellation, that were a billion light years away and that the light from these remote stellar objects had started its journey to their telescopes around the time mankind was beginning to evolve from the primordial sludge on Earth.

Bold Street Time Warp

The following story is an account of a man who inadvertently strolled into the past early in July 1996 in Liverpool city centre. Frank, an off-duty policeman from Melling and his wife, Carol, were in Liverpool shopping one Saturday afternoon. At Central Station, the couple split up. Carol set off to what was then Dillons Bookshop in Bold Street to purchase a copy of Irvine Welsh's book, *Trainspotting*, while Frank headed for a record store in Ranelagh Street, to look for a CD. About 20 minutes later, he was walking up the incline near the Lyceum, which emerges in Bold Street, intending to meet up with his wife in the bookshop, when he suddenly noticed that he had somehow entered an oasis of quietness.

Suddenly, a small box-shaped van, that looked like something out of the 1950s, sped across his path, sounding its horn as it narrowly missed him. Frank noted that the van had the name 'Caplan's' emblazoned on its side. When the policeman looked down at the ground, he noticed that he was standing in the road. He immediately thought that this was strange, because the last time he had seen the bottom of Bold Street, it had been pedestrianised.

Frank crossed the road and was immediately struck by the fact that Dillons bookshop was no longer there. In its place, stood a store with the name 'Cripps' over its two entrances. He was understandably confused. He peered into the window of Cripps and found no books on display. They had been replaced by a large collection of women's handbags and shoes.

The policeman scanned the street and saw that the people were wearing clothes that would have been worn in the 1940s and 50s, which really unnerved him. He realised that he had somehow walked into the Bold Street of 40-odd years ago. Suddenly, Frank caught sight of a girl of about 20, dressed in the clothes of a mid-1990s girl; hipsters and a lime-coloured sleeveless top and he breathed a sigh of relief. The bag she carried had the name Miss Selfridge on it, which helped to reassure him that he was still somehow partly in 1996, but it was still a paradox. He smiled at the girl as she walked past him and entered Cripps.

As he followed her through the entrance, the whole interior of the building changed in a flash to that of Dillons bookshop. The policeman was back in his own time. Without considering his actions, he grabbed the girl by the arm.

"Did you see that?" he asked her.

"Yeah. I thought it was a new shop that had just opened. I was going in to look at the clothes, but it's a bookshop," she said, calmly.

She then just laughed, shook her head and walked back out again. Frank later described how the girl had looked back and shaken her head again in disbelief. When he told his wife about the incident, she said that she had not noticed anything strange, but Frank was really adamant that he had not hallucinated the episode.

I gave an account of this strange timeslip on the *Billy Butler Show*. Within minutes, people were ringing in to the station to confirm that, in the late 1950s and early 1960s, there had been a store called Cripps, situated in the exact location where Dillons bookshop now stood; there had also been a local firm called Caplan's in existence around the same time. What's more, I also received letters and telephone calls from listeners who had also experienced strange things in the same part of Bold Street where the policeman had stepped into another era.

A man who worked on the renovation of the Lyceum building in Bold Street, said that his digital watch went backwards for two hours one day. On another occasion, he put down his safety helmet and when he looked down, literally seconds later, it had vanished, yet no one was within 50 feet of him.

Emma Black, a Radio Merseyside listener, sent me a fascinating cutting from a 1970s magazine, concerning a timeslip which apparently allowed a telephone conversation to take place between two people spaced 30 years apart. The following summary of this strange story may seem like an episode of *The Twilight Zone*, but I have heard of three other similar cases.

There's a War On!

An old woman named Alma Bristow of Bidston, tried to ring her sister (who had recently lost her husband) in Frodsham, Cheshire. Alma always had difficulty dialling numbers on the old British Telecom analogue telephone, because she suffered from stabbing arthritis in her fingers. Alma had evidently mis-dialled her sister's number, as a man's voice answered.

"Captain Hamilton here," he said.

Alma asked if her sister was there, but Hamilton cut her short.

"This is not a civilian number," he replied haughtily. "Who are you?"

Alma gave her name and, as she did so, she heard a sound at the other end of the telephone that she had not heard since she was a young woman: an air-raid siren sounding.

"Sounds like World War Two over there," she joked.

There was an uncomfortable pause, then Captain Hamilton replied, "What are you talking about?"

"The air-raid siren. Sounds like the war's still on," Alma said, about to hang up.

"Of course the war's still on. Where did you get my number from?" said Hamilton, growing steadily more exasperated.

"The war ended years ago, in 1945," said Alma rationally, suspecting she was a victim of the *Candid Camera Show*.

Captain Hamilton could be heard whispering to an associate, before resuming the surreal conversation.

"It isn't 1945 yet. If we trace you, you'll be thrown into prison for this lark you know. You're wasting valuable time, woman."

"Eh? It's 1974. The war's been over for years," Alma retorted.

Then she heard the unmistakable rumble of bombing coming over the telephone. "We'll deal with you later, make no mistake!" said Captain Hamilton, slamming down the phone down. Alma listened eagerly for him to pick up the handset of his telephone once again, but he never did. Alma never knew if she had been the victim of an elaborate hoax, or whether she had really had talked with someone from wartime Britain.

The two previous stories about timeslips suggest that the events of the past are still going on somewhere along the fourth dimension. Is it not ironic how the clock rules all our lives, yet we know virtually nothing about time itself? Our ignorance regarding the nature of time reminds me of a thought-provoking remark which Einstein once made: "What does a fish know about the water in which he swims all his life?"

Ghostly Places

Getting into the Spirit of Things ...

A lot of people have asked me if there are any haunted places where ghosts can be seen. Well, there are plenty of sites across the north west that are said to be haunted, although I obviously cannot guarantee that a ghost will make an appearance at any particular time. Here is a selection which you may like to visit:

Speke Hall is well worth a look. For hundreds of years a white lady has been seen walking through the Tapestry Room. No one knows who she is, but she has been seen by hundreds of people over the years. Speke Hall is open Tuesday to Sunday and Bank Holiday Monday as well.

Chingle Hall, just north of Preston near Goosnargh, was built in 1258 from the wood of the Viking vessels that had sunk in the River Ribble. Chingle Hall was one of the last strongholds of the Catholic faith during the Reformation and many priests were killed there after being caught celebrating secret masses. The place has four secret passages where the priests once hid. It is said to be haunted by several ghosts, one of whom is renowned for giving a friendly pat on the back, but the others are terrifying and have allegedly even attacked tourists. In one instance, one visitor felt an icy hand around his neck and was then flung across the room by an invisible force. A grotesque face has also been spotted, looking out of the windows of the hall.

St Oswald's Church. Each Sunday in St Oswald's Church in Ashton-in-Makerfield, you can see the Holy Hand: a small shrivelled hand encased in a glass casket, which is claimed to possess miraculous powers. It is the hand of St Edmund Arrowsmith, who was martyred in 1628. The Holy Hand is said to have been curing people from 1736 and many pilgrims still visit the church simply to see it. The 372-year-old hand really is a most unusual spectacle.

Over the years, in addition to the hand, many visitors to the church have also witnessed the ghost of an old highwayman, seen slowly wandering about in the graveyard.

Bidston Hill. Across the water at Bidston Hill, near Birkenhead, there is a flat, sandstone outcrop close to Bidston Conservatory, where you can see several mysterious carvings which are around a thousand years old. There are carvings of a moon goddess, with a cat's head, and a horse which exactly faces midsummer sunrise. This area of Bidston Hill was venerated as a mystical gateway to another world in ancient times and many UFO researchers confirm that the area has an unusually high incidence of UFO sightings.

Caution for the Curious

The budding ghost hunter must remember that he is dabbling in a very serious subject. Investigating the paranormal should not be regarded as just another hobby like stamp-collecting, or bird-watching. Delving into an unknown phenomenon, which our present science cannot explain, requires a cool head and a genuine inquisitiveness, tempered with logic. There are many well-reported horror stories of certain frivolous individuals toying about with ouija boards and later discovering that they have unleashed all sorts of negative malevolent forces upon themselves. The fate of such meddlers is often psychological illness. So, if you have no genuine interest in the supernatural sphere, beyond sensationalism, think again, because there is a very dark side to the subject.

To find a ghost to investigate is quite a simple matter. Statistically, quite a high percentage of the population (actually one in six, to be precise) has had a paranormal experience, so the number of people who know someone who has seen something strange makes it likely that you will often learn of a haunting through word-of-mouth contact. Three other good sources are the local press, regional television news programmes and the local radio bulletin. A browse through the local history section of a good bookshop will obviously also be helpful.

Alternatively, you could join the Society of Psychical Research, who have extensive archives of hauntings all over the country and, in fact, the world. Once you have found the place where a ghost is reputed to haunt, you must adopt the same methods which the police use in a criminal enquiry. Record (by tape if possible) the description of the ghost given by any witnesses and take down basic details, such as the date, the exact place and time where the apparition was seen etc. If several people claim to have witnessed a ghost, interview them all separately and out of ear-shot of one another, to compare the described events.

Ask them what they were doing, or thinking, at the time of the sighting and even question them about their frame of mind before and after the occurrence. Also, take a careful look around the room or area where the ghost was seen and ask the witness or witnesses if they have noticed any objects which have been moved or damaged. Then, make a rough sketch of the place where the ghost stood and if it moved about, draw its route or trajectory.

If you are granted permission to lie in wait for the ghost on the premises, here is a list of some useful equipment:

Notebook and pens – for obvious reasons.

Camera – probably a single-lens-reflex model with a short focus (wide-angle) lens, loaded with a roll of fast film (ASA 400 upwards). Using a flash is not recommended, as the high luminosity can impair eyes that have adapted to the dark. If possible, mount the camera on a tripod and position it so that most of the room is in the shot. Take a few snaps of the room. Not only will this provide a photographic record, you may actually capture an image of a ghost even though it was not visible at the time.

You may also like to experiment with infra-red film, which is sensitive to the invisible radiation at the end of the visible electromagnetic spectrum. But remember, because infra-red is a long-wave form of radiation, the focusing is different and you will need an infra-red filter. If in doubt, consult your camera manual, or any good photographic dealer.

If you don't fancy waiting around for the ghost to turn up, there are things called capacitance switches that can be attached to the camera. These devices will trigger the camera by electronically sensing the approach of a human or animal. Allegedly, they sometimes also react to ghosts.

If you have the resources and the ingenuity, you could set up a cine camera (with fast film), or a portable video camera and wire them to capacitance switches. Then there is the exciting possibility of capturing moving images of an apparition.

Tape recorder – for quality, use a reel-to-reel one if affordable, otherwise, the good old portable cassette recorder will do, loaded with a C120 low-noise cassette. An external microphone will produce better results than the recorder's built-in condenser mike, which has the annoying habit of picking up the noise produced by the electric motor of the tape itself

Like the camera, the tape can be left to go off by itself, by either attaching a capacitance switch to it, or by attaching a pre-set electronic timer to the tape's REM socket. Alternatively, you can attach a darkness-activated switch to the tape via its REM socket. This will activate the tape recorder as soon as night falls, which is when things have a reputation for going bump!

If you can afford one, use a stereo tape recorder so that, upon playback, the direction the recorded noise originated from can be determined. If an ultrasonic transducer is plugged into the MIC socket, you may be able to record sounds outside the range of human hearing.

Thermometer – preferably a digital one, otherwise the old analogue type with a column of alcohol or mercury will do. Before, during and after any supernatural occurrence, take a note of the room temperature. A drop in temperature is a widely-reported indication of an impending materialisation.

Pressure pads – purchased from most electronic component stores, the pads, usually the size of a small mat, can activate a circuit when pressure is applied to them (for example standing on them) and are manufactured to be used in burglar alarms. A schematic circuit can be devised for an alarm that can be attached to a pressure mat. Pads will also indicate the presence of hoaxers!

Magnetic compass – this is useful to determine if there is any link with the appearance of a ghost and disruptions in the earth's magnetic field. For the dedicated investigator, a device called a magnetometer can accurately measure any magnetic anomaly.

Reel of cotton thread – stretch a thread of cotton across a room where a ghost is known to walk, to ascertain its solidity.

Watch – either an analogue watch with a luminous dial or a digital one with a back-lit display. If possible, use a stopwatch to measure the exact duration of a paranormal occurrence.

Torch – a red piece of filter paper over the torch will help you consult your notebook or equipment in the dark without impairing your night vision.

Masking tape – this can be placed along the edges of doors and windows to prevent hoaxers moving into the area being observed.

Fluorescent powder – this can be scattered around the immediate area of the haunting. If any hoaxer sneaks across the area, the powder will glow on his or her shoes when illuminated by an ultra-violet lamp.

Also, researching the history of a haunted premises is essential, unless the ghost under investigation is the result of a recent death and has been positively identified by those people who knew the deceased, such as family and friends.

To dig up information on the history of a property the best place to start is the Central Library, where you can look up the address of the haunted house in the electoral register. This register, which was first compiled in 1832, is a list of all the people in the city who are entitled to vote. The register is published every year on 15 February and it gives the name and address of each elector.

Another good source of information is the church. For hundreds of years the church has been required to keep records of baptisms, marriages and burials. These records are usually written (sometimes in Latin) by the minister and his church warden. For instance, in the register of the Holy Trinity Church at Stratford there is an entry which reads, 'Gulielmus filius Johannes Shakspere' which, when translated means, 'William son of John Shakespeare'.

A basic knowledge of local history is obviously going to be an advantage to you if you are a budding ghost-hunter, so you should read as much on the subject as you can until you can mentally visualise what life was like in the different historical periods. Consult the old street maps of your local region and compare them with modern ones, also visit the local museum.

You should familiarise yourself with the different architectural periods. Pick an old house that you have seen and guess when it was built, then go and read up on it and see how close your guess was. Do the same with old furniture and other antique household objects. You do not have to study until you have the knowledge of an expert, just to the point where you can recognise the period to which an object belongs.

And Finally ...

This touching letter was sent to me at Radio Merseyside in August 1996, from a young listener in Truro Road, Wavertree. I have reproduced it here exactly as it was written:

Dear Tom,

My name is Leonie. I am 9 years old. I seen a ghost when I was 6. It was black and it was not on the ground. I was scared. My Mum was upstairs. I ran upstairs and told my Mum. Me and my Mum went downstairs and we put candiles where I seen the ghcst. I new it would not come back but I was still scared. I had to stay off school for three days and wen I was in school I was still a bit scared but I new it would not come back, I am 9 years old now and I have not seen it since and I am glad.

from Leonie

So it seems that anyone, any age, anywhere has the potential to experience paranormal activity. This child's blunt account has a genuine honesty which certainly raises the query of just what is out there?

If you have had a paranormal encounter, or a supernatural experience of any sort, please drop a line to

Thomas Slemen
c/o Bluecoat Press
Bluecoat Chambers
14 School Lane
Liverpool L1 3BX

All correspondence will be answered.